AF005

MASSIMILIANO AFIERO

AXIS FORCES
5

WW2 AXIS
FORCES

The Axis Forces 005 - First edition January 2018 by Soldiershop.com.
Cover & Art Design by soldiershop factory.   ISBN code: 978-88-93273077

In merito alla specifica serie Italia storia ebook serie Ritterkreuz l'editore Soldiershop informa che non essendone l'autore ne il primo editore del materiale pervenuto dall'associazione Ritterkreuz, declina ogni responsabilità in merito al suo contenuto di testi e/o immagini e la sua correttezza. A tal proposito segnaliamo che la pubblicazione Ritterkreuz tratta esclusivamente argomenti a carattere storico-militare e non intende esaltare alcun tipo di ideologia politica presente o del passato cosi come non intende esaltare alcun tipo di regime politico del secolo precedente ed alcuna forma di razzismo.

Note editoriali dell'edizione cartacea

The Axis Forces number 5 – January 2018

Direction and editing
Via San Giorgio, 11 – 80021 Afragola (NA) - ITALY
Managing and Chief Editor: Massimiliano Afiero
Email: maxafiero@libero.it - **Website**: www.maxafiero.it

Contributors

Stefano Canavassi, Carlos Caballero Jurado, Rene Chavez, Carlo Cucut, Daniel Fanni, Dmitry Frolov, Antonio Guerra, John B. Köser, Lars Larsen, Christophe Leguérandais, Eduardo M. Gil Martínez, Peter Mooney, Erik Norling, Raphael Riccio, Marc Rikmenspoel, Johannes Scharf, Charles Trang, Cesare Veronesi, Sergio Volpe

Editorial

Happy 2018 to all, hoping deeply and with all my heart that this new year may hold many good and positive things for everyone and that it may increase the worldwide awareness of our magazine. This is the second year of activity and we hope to continue to grow, improving our magazine along with your fundamental support. To this end, I invite all our readers, who surf the Internet and are enrolled in various military history forums, to publicize our publication and post comments regarding it. Thank you all for your cooperation thus far. As for the contents, we have followed your suggestions and we are trying to widen the topics to all Axis nations and to all foreign volunteer units, trying to deal with unpublished topics and subjects that have not yet been adequately addressed by official historiography. In this new issue, we continue to talk about the use of the SS units on the Narva front, we continue with an excerpt from a new book dedicated to the memories of Georg Diers during the fighting in Berlin, the first part of an article dedicated to enrollment of the Albanian volunteers in the Waffen SS, the employment of V./LSSAH on the Leningrad front, the first part of a comprehensive work on the Hungarian armored units on the Eastern front and ending with an article on the decorations awarded to the Italian soldiers who fought in Russia. Happy New Year to all and see you in the next issue.

Massimiliano Afiero

Contents

The battle for Narva, 1944
by Massimiliano Afiero – 2nd part

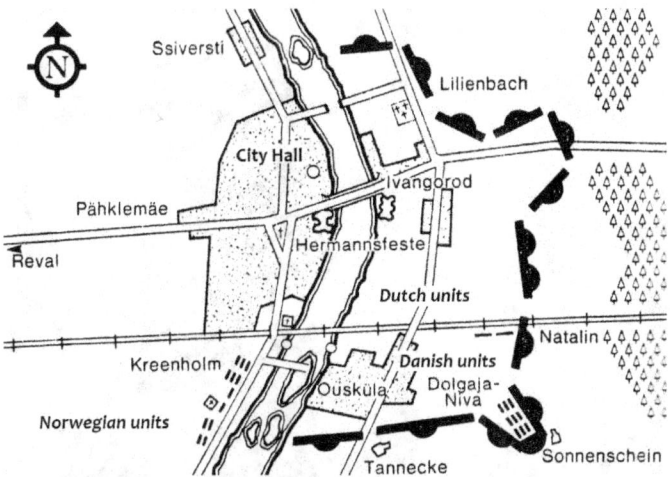

The Narva bridgehead with Lilienbach's position.

German soldiers in a night attack in the snow, March 1944.

Dutch soldiers in movement within the bridgehead.

The fighting for Lilienbach continued for another two days during which the Dutch regiment *"de Ruyter"* suffered serious losses. Among the dead was the commander of II Battalion, *SS-Hstuf.* Burmester. Enemy penetrations, defensive actions and counterattacks followed in rapid succession, completely tiring out the already exhausted Dutch volunteers. Commander Hans Collani wondered just how much longer his valorous grenadiers would be able to hold out under those trying conditions.

New attacks

The enemy artillery continued savagely punish the positions of the Dutch volunteers in the bridgehead. In the end, it was decided to abandon the Lilienbach position, which was judged to be too exposed to enemy fire and attacks. The Dutch units withdrew to a new positon known as "the Devil's Meadow" (*Teufelwiese* in German). During the night between 13 and 14 March, the Soviets lost no time in attacking the new position, catching the Dutch units, who were still setting up their new positions, by surprise. The new commander of *II./de Ruyter*, *SS-Hstuf.* Walter Diener was killed during the defensive fighting. Another company commander was wounded while leading a counterattack. The commander of a nearby company, the 7th, *SS-Ostuf*. Helmut Scholz, seeing the seriousness of the situation, immediately organized a counterattack with a few courageous volunteers, and with the force born of desperation was able to throw the enemy from their positions.

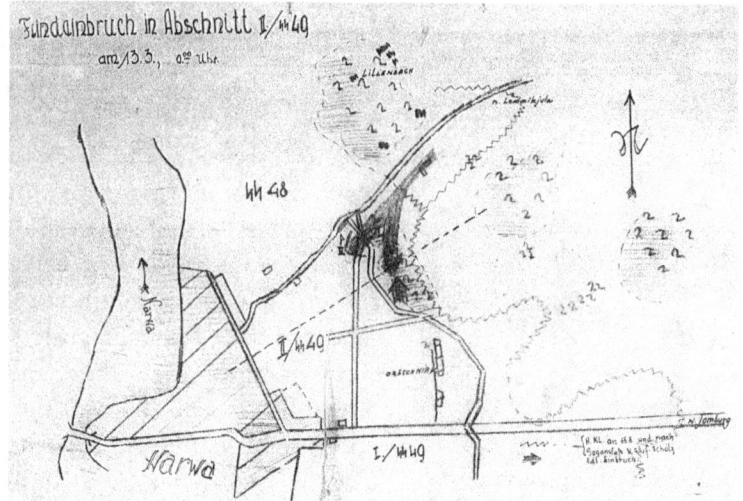

Map of Scholz's action attached to the citation for the *Ritterkreuz*.

SS-Ostuf. Helmut Scholz.

Waffen SS soldiers on Narva front, March 1944.

The next day the regimental adjutant, *SS-Ustuf*. Karl-Heinz Ertel, assumed temporary command of *II./de Ruyter*, before handing it over a few days later to *SS-Hstuf*. Karl-Heinz Frühauf. The valor and efforts of the Dutch volunteers were mentioned in the *Oberkommando der Wehrmacht* report of 15 March 1944: "...*During the final days of combat in the northern sector of the eastern front, the Dutch regiment "General Seyffardt" of the* SS "Nederland" Brigade *distinguished itself particularly under the command of* SS-Ostubaf. *Jörchel*". After further local attacks, a new extraordinary Soviet artillery barrage was unleashed on the hill at Lilienbach and on the "Devil's Meadow" during the day of 22 March. The positions of the 5th Company of *SS-Ostuf*. Helmut Hirt were literally pulverized. The Soviets attacked soon after with infantry. *SS-Hstuf*. Frühauf, having collected all of the men that were available, including grenadiers, messengers and radiomen, led a desperate counterattack against enemy units that had been able to penetrate the forward positions. The action came close to failing several times because of the enemy's superior numbers, but Frühauf knew how to courageously lead his men in the attack and in the end was able to retake all of the positions that had been lost.

German grenadiers moving in the trenches in the sector of Narva.

SS-Hstuf. Frühauf.

Ivangorod fortress and *Waffen SS* soldiers.

The *'Bunse'* brigde at Narva, March 1944.

Scholz and Frühauf played a decisive role in the defense of the bridgehead during the month of March. The *Nederland* artillery pieces commanded by *SS-Stubaf.* Wilhelm Schlüter, which remained emplaced north of the main supply line, continued to be hard pressed to hold back the attacks of Soviet units during this period.

Festung Narva

On 23 March 1944, Hitler officially proclaimed *Festung Narva*, or Fortress Narva. Because Narva had been designated as a fortress city it therefore had to be defended at all costs. For the defenders this meant that while everyone else was able to abandon their positions, they had to remain at their posts and risk ending up as prisoners of the Soviets or, at worst, to be killed. *Nordland* and

Nederland had already contributed to the defense of the city, paying a high price in blood, suffering overall losses of about 7,500 men, calculated beginning in December 1943. During the same period, the *SS Nederland* Brigade had received only 1,336 replacements, which were the previously cited survivors of the two *Luftwaffe* field divisions that had been disbanded after the terrible fighting at Oranienbaum.

Waffen SS defensive position in the Narva sector, March 1944: in the trenches, SS trooper keeps the vigil while comrades try to get some sleep standing and wrapped in their blankets.

SS-Brigdf. **Wagner** and *SS-Stubaf.* **Ziemssen.**

With the arrival of the spring season and the beginning of the thaw, the front stabilized during the months of April and May, except for long-distance artillery duels, aircraft encounters, and clashes between reconnaissance patrols. As of 13 April, the overall losses of the *Nederland* Brigade amounted to 87 officers (dead, wounded and missing), 502 NCOs and 3,139 soldiers. Effective strength of the Brigade had thus fallen to 6,305 from an initial strength figure of 9,342.

On 20 April, the commander of the Dutch SS Brigade as well as of *"Festung Narva"*, Jürgen Wagner, was promoted to the rank of *SS-Brigadeführer und Generalmajor der Waffen-SS*. Wagner also chose a new Chief of Staff (Ia), as on 6 May *SS-Stubaf.* Ziemssen had been temporarily removed from his position by order of Himmler, in order to attend a training course. *SS-Hauptsturmführer* Helmut Kordts took his place. On 21 April 1944, the commander of *SS-Freiw.Pz.Gr.Rgt. 48 "General Seyffardt"*, Wolfgang Jörchel, was awarded the Knight's Cross for the exemplary performance by his men during the defensive battles at the Narva bridgehead.

SS-Ostubaf. **Jörchel (Left) decorated with the Knight's Cross by** *SS-Brigdf.* **Wagner.**

SS-Ustuf. **Hermann Schoofs.**

On 24 April, several officers of the Dutch Brigade were presented with the German Cross in Gold: the recipients were *SS-Ostubaf.* Collani, commander of the 49th SS Regiment, *SS-Hstuf.* Walter Diener (posthumously), commander of *II./de Ruyter*, *SS-Ostuf.* Hans Robert Jauss (*4./General Seyffardt*) and *SS-Ustuf.* Hermann Schoofs, adjutant of *Pionier-Bataillon 54*. In early May, *SS-Ostubaf.* Jörchel was designated as the new commander of the *SS-Junkerschule* at Prague, which resulted in command of the *General Seyffardt* Regiment being assumed at first by *SS-Sturmbannführer* Herbert Garthe and later, at the beginning of July, by *SS-Ostubaf.* Richard Benner, coming from the *SS-Division Nord*. In the following weeks, the defensive battles along the entire length of the front continued and increased in intensity, although the Soviets were unable to make any gains worthy of note. The Germanic volunteers of the *Waffen SS* continued to stubbornly defend their positions without giving up an inch of ground to the enemy. During the months of April and May, the commander of the III SS Armored Corps, *SS-Ogruf.* Felix Steiner and the commander of the *Heeresgruppe*

Nord, General Friessner, often visited the Dutch positions, complimenting Wagner on the exemplary conduct of his men. During this period, the Dutch volunteers were trained in the use of new individual anti-tank weapons, the *Panzerfaust* and *Panzerschreck*. The first of these proved to be a formidable anti-tank weapon especially when fighting in urban areas, and was capable of penetrating the thick armor of the Soviet tanks.

SS-Brigadeführer and Generalmajor of the *Waffen-SS* Jürgen Wagner (left), relaxing with newly decorated Iron Cross 2nd class winners, May 1944.

A *Panzerschreck* on a defensive position at Narva.

A German *MG-42* repelling an enemy attack.

The *Panzerschreck* was instead the German version of the American bazooka and in contrast to the *Panzerfaust* needed a team of two men in order to be employed properly in the field: one soldier manned the weapon and another soldier loaded it from behind. Large numbers of these anti-tank weapons were delivered to the Dutch SS Brigade. On 20 May 1944, *SS-Obf.* Kurt Brasack left command of the *Nederland* Brigade's artillery regiment because he was reassigned to *IV.SS-Pz.Korps*, with command of the artillery unit passing to *SS-Stubaf.* Schlüter, former commander of *III./Art.Rgt.4* of the *SS Polizei* Division.

Dutch volunteer with *PPSh-41*.

A new Soviet offensive

During the month of June, *Festung Narva* continued to hold up against enemy attacks. On 12 June 1944, the Soviets launched a new massive offensive all along the *Panther* line. In the afternoon of that same day, the area of Narva found itself once again under a hurricane of fire. The Dutch volunteers, who were deployed in the north-eastern sector of the bridgehead, burrowed into their bunkers to escape the hail of fire and steel. From his command post in the *Hermannfeste*, Wagner apprehensively followed the unfolding situation. The first assault by the Soviet infantry was unleashed around 16:15, north of the Dolgaja-Niva railway line, in the southern sector of the bridgehead. The shelling against the northern sector had only been a diversion. When all communications with the *Danmark* Regiment broke down, there was complete chaos. Around 17:20 word was received that the Soviets had passed at Dolgaja-Niva. The reserves of the Dutch Brigade, which had already been put on alert, were committed immediately. Support was provided by artillery fire from *Nordland* and *Nederland*, as well as by a handful of *Sturmgeschützen*. At 17:56 the positions at Dolgaja-Niva and Sonnenschein were once again in German hands.

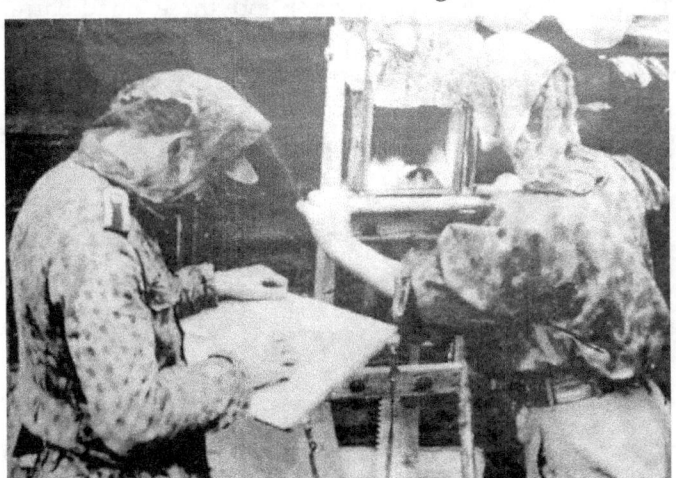

Waffen SS soldiers on defensive positions on Narva front, Spring 1944.

The Soviets renewed the attack about an hour later. At 19:06 Wagner received word that the position at Sonnenschein, which was the southernmost outpost of the bridgehead, had been captured by the Soviets. A new counterattack was planned for 19:35. At 21:35, *SS-Stubaf.* Krügel reported that the counterattack was under way. Meanwhile, north of Sonnenschein other Soviet units were attempting to break through the *HKL* (*HauptKampfLinie*), the main combat line. The *Waffen SS* soldiers were able to stop this new attack with the fire from machine guns, while *Panzerfaust* teams took care of the tanks. At 23:35, Sonnenschein was returned to German hands.

German soldiers defending the Estonian bank of the Narva River with the fortress of Ivangorod on the opposite side, Summer 1944.

On 19 June, *SS-Stubaf*. Wolfgang Grosch, a special envoy of Himmler's, reached the bridgehead. The *Reichsführer* wanted Narva to serve as an example to all of the German Army. Grosch presented Wagner with a plan of Himmler's to continue to defend the bridgehead to the last and to push back the Soviets. But on that very same day a number of assault guns were transferred from *Nederland* to *Nordland*. Only two *Panther* tanks and ten *Sturmgeschützen* remained under command of the *Nederland* Brigade. Following the death of Shock, *SS-Panzerjäger-Abteilung 54* had come under the command of *SS-Hstuf*. Paul Krauss. To compensate to some extent for the loss of the assault guns, the initial elements of *II./SS-Art.Rgt. 4* finally arrived from Beneschau, consisting of a few guns (*leichte Feldhaubitze 18*, which were light field howitzers) and three quad-barrel *Flakvierling* anti-aircraft guns. The guns and the *Flakvierling* were unloaded at Suur-Soldino and from there were transferred to the front at Narva.

A *Flakvierling* in action.

A gunner of the Dutch SS Brigade standing by his gun.

German field artillery firing.

The new artillery group was commanded by *SS-Ustuf*. Fritz Topeters, while the *Flakzug* (the platoon with the "quad" guns), which was subordinate to the artillery regiment, was commanded by *SS-Ustuf*. Willi Krämer. The *Flak* guns were quickly employed against the

Soviet air attacks that were concentrated against the main bridge over the Narva River, near the textile factory west of Natalin.

Narva after artillery and air raids (*National Archives of Norway*).

On 20 June 1944, Soviet artillery resumed its shelling of the Dutch positions for the entire day. However, there were no attacks by the enemy infantry.

Operation Urlaubsperre

Encouraged by the continuing defensive successes by his men, in an attempt to ease the enemy pressure and to somehow raise the morale of the troops who had for months been engaged in a wearying passive defense posture, *SS-Brigdf.* Wagner conceived a limited offensive action with the objective of shifting the defensive line more to the east, along the line that ran from Narva to the area east of Lilienbach. The operation was assigned the code name *Urlaubsperre* (end of the vacation).

German 88mm gun firing.

However, before launching the attack, Wagner sent out many reconnaissance patrols in order to determine the precise locations of enemy firing positions and the strength of the forces that were facing him. To that end, on 23

June, a platoon of Dutch volunteers entered no-man's land with the aim of taking prisoners in order to obtain intelligence from them. However, before they could complete their mission the SS grenadiers realized, too late, that they had strayed into an enemy minefield. As soon as the first volunteer triggered a mine, all hell broke loose. The Soviets quickly opened fire with their mortars. A group of Dutchmen managed to take cover in several enemy trenches that had been abandoned and stayed there until dusk fell. When it became dark, the group was able to return safe and sound to friendly lines. This reconnaissance operation thus closed with nothing to show for it, and as Wagner wrote in the Brigade diary, with *"Erhebliche Verlust"*, that is, with significant losses.

SS-Gruf. von Scholz (Right) with one of his officers.

SS-Brigdf. Jürgen Wagner.

Waffen SS defensive positions at Narva.

On 25 June, Wagner reported for a conference with von Scholz, commanding *Nordland*, to discuss operational plans. Both agreed that a mixed combat group should be employed, consisting of units from *Nederland* and from *Nordland*. It was therefore decided that Dutch 48th SS Regiment *General Seyffardt* would form the leading element, supported by *III./Norge* along with *SS-Pionier-Bataillon 11* (the *Nordland* engineer battalion). Supporting fire would be provided by the artillery of both units. On Wagner's orders, small groups of soldiers began a series of "instigating" actions along the entire Narva front in order to deceive the Soviets as to where the counterattack would actually take place. Despite all of these preparations, in the end the operation was cancelled, mainly due to the lack of information on the true strength of the enemy forces. It should also be noted that only a few days earlier, on 22 June, the Soviets had begun a large offensive against the German Army Group Center (Operation *Bagration*) in order to separate it from Army Group North. Once the central front fell, the German forces in the Baltics risked being completely isolated. Contemporaneous Soviet attacks in Karelia on the Finnish front were about to cause Finland to capitulate, posing an even greater threat to the entire Estonian front. Isolated at the tip of the northern front, Narva was by now indefensible.

On 22 June 1944, the Soviets had begun a large offensive...

German soldiers defending from an enemy attack.

Within the German high command, plans were being made for its abandonment, despite the fact that by now the city had become the symbol of resistance by the European volunteers against the Soviet forces.

Abandoning Narva

In early July, the units of *Nederland* and *Nordland* were again engaged in the area of Dolgaja-Niva, repelling new enemy attacks. On 8 July, grenadiers from *General Seyffardt* and *Danmark* were caught up in a furious defensive battle that did not end until late at night, with heavy losses on both sides. On 11 July 1944, the southern wing of the German 18th Army was attacked by Soviet forces of the Second Baltic Front; this caused a general retreat of German forces to the west. Consequently, *III.SS-Panzer-Korps* also received the order to pull back about twenty kilometers from Narva along a new defensive line designated *Tannenbergstellung*, along the Narva-Riga road; the name Tannenberg commemorated the great German victory in 1914, against the Czarist army. Naturally the withdrawal movement required time to execute and above all required the sacrifice by several units which had to remain as a rear guard to cover the withdrawal in good order by all of the other units. The Dutch units were committed to that mission and while the *"de Ruyter"* Regiment commanded by *SS-Ostubaf.* Collani was able to disengage following some tough fighting, the *General Seyffardt* Regiment under Benner was not able to break off contact and was surrounded by the enemy.

Waffen-SS **soldiers on Narva Front, Summer 1944.**

SS-Ostubaf. **Hans Collani.**

SS-Ostubaf. **Alfons Rebane.**

On 19 July 1944, in an official communique addressed to the Brigade, General Steiner again complimented the Dutch volunteers for their combat successes in the defense around Narva: *"...The exceptional behavior of the troops and the strong leadership of the* Nederland *Brigade commanders deserve limitless recognition. I thank both for their valorous courage that they have demonstrated until now"*.

The Soviets returned to attack the bridgehead on 24 July, as always preceded by the usual preparatory artillery fire. That same day, by order of Hitler, General Friessner was replaced as commander of *Heeresgruppe Nord* by General Schörner, who arrived in Narva while it was under enemy attack. The *Nederland* units that were engaged in covering the withdrawal of the other German units towards the *Tannenbergstellung* had been reinforced by other units including the II Battalion of the 47th Estonian SS Regiment commanded by *SS-Stubaf.* Alfons Rebane, a coast artillery detachment from Hungerburg, and a *Pak* platoon from the 20th Estonian SS Division. Their mission remained defense of the far northern secor of the bridgehead, from the center of Narva to Hungerburg on the Baltic coast. To the south were units from *Nordland* reinforced by part of *Panzer Abteilung 11 Hermann von Salza*, the *Gruppe Riipalu* (the staff of the 45th Estonian Regiment), the reinforced 5th Company of the 48th Dutch SS Regiment, known as the *"Seyffardt"*, and a section of *SS-Panzer Jäger Abteilung 20*. The *III.SS-Panzer Korps* units that comprised the rear guard remained in the city. *SS-Hstuf.* Wanhöfer, commander of *SS-Pionier Bataillon 54*, arranged to blow all of the bridges over the Narva River. Only one of the bridges was left still standing because the charges did not ignite.

German soldiers cross a wooden bridge in Narva, Summer 1944.   *SS-Hstuf.* **Wanhöfer.**

Waffen SS **soldiers in Narva, 1944.**

Luckily Wanhöfer was still on the scene *"…Damn it all! The bridge must not remain intact. The enemy's forward elements can pass without a problem!"* he shouted to his men. New charges had to be placed, so Wanhöfer ordered his driver to: *"go immediately to Petri Square! Get as much explosives as you can carry and get back here as quickly as possible!"*. While awaiting the return of the little *Kübelwagen* with its new load of explosives, a squad of Dutch engineers took up the defense of the bridge itself, which was already under fire from Soviet mortars. The *Kübelwagen* returned shortly thereafter and the engineers placed the explosive charges, all the while under enemy fire. Their other comrades provided covering fire, and the new charges were soon set in place. After all of the men had taken cover, the bridge was blown up with a tremendous roar. When the Soviets reached the bank of the river they found not a single intact bridge. That same day of 25 July, the *"General Seyffardt"*, the *II./de Ruyter*, and the *7./Danmark* were still in Narva. The artillery forward observers were still in place, while new emplacements for the batteries of *III.SS-Pz.Korps* were being established further to the west. Soviet aircraft again bombed the city, destroying the few ruins that had still been left standing. In the early afternoon, *SS-Hstuf.* Wanhöfer and his engineers moved to the west aboard three vehicles to reach the new positions established for the assembly of the units. The Soviets were by now very close. For his excellent actions during the fighting for Narva, Wanhöfer was awarded the Knight's Cross on 27 August 1944. On 25 July, the second day of the Soviet offensive, in the area around Vasa, north of Narva where the Estonian SS units were deployed, the enemy was able to achieve a dangerous breakthrough.

Waffen SS soldiers prepare to leave their positions in Narva, Summer 1944.

SS-Brigdf. Fritz von Scholz.

Around 10:50, *SS-Brigdadeführer* Jürgen Wagner, who was still firmly entrenched in his command post, received news that units of the 20th Estonian SS Division had begun to pull back, thereby leaving the northern sector undefended. Because of this, units from *Nederland* had to hurry to close the dangerous gap at Hungerburg; the units included grenadiers of the 48th SS Regiment and I Battalion of the 49th, along with other Army units. This meant a new defensive battle calling for extreme sacrifice to protect the withdrawal of other German units. These continual rear-guard covering actions in the end proved to be fatal to the Dutch SS detachments.

The Dutch retreat

In fact, when *II./de Ruyter* and units of "*General Seyffardt*" finally began to withdraw to the west, they soon found their route blocked by Soviet units that had already come from Vanaküla. The Dutch volunteers prepared to fight their last battle during that tragic retreat. Along with Benner's regiment were other units: the *7./Danmark*, the *II./de Ruyter*, the *Bataillon Rebane* of the *20.SS-Division*, the *Nederland* disciplinary platoon[1], and *SS-Panzer-Jäger Abteilung 54* (minus one battery).

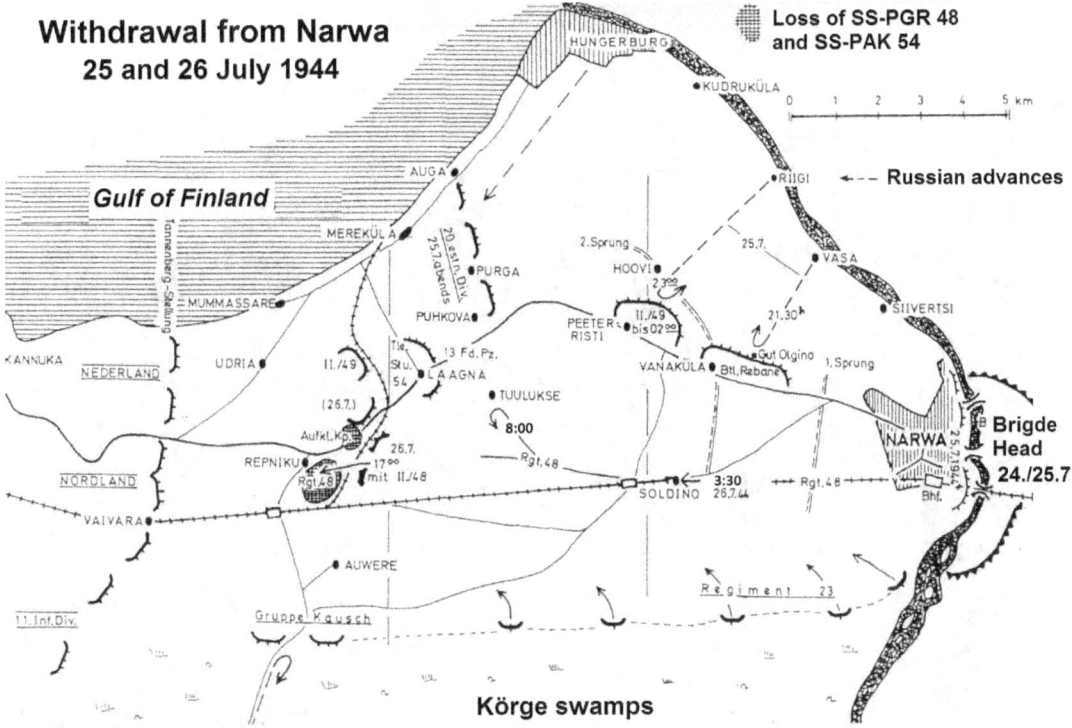

Withdrawal from Narwa
25 and 26 July 1944

Loss of SS-PGR 48 and SS-PAK 54

Gulf of Finland

Körge swamps

SS-Ostubaf. **Richard Benner.**

The withdrawal of the units had been planned by phases, after having established several intermediate positions to be occupied as the maneuver was being carried out. On the regiment's left was the *Bataillon Rebane*, and on the right was *II./de Ruyter*. *SS-Ostubaf.* Benner had assumed command of the regiment only a few days earlier, and coming from the Finnish front from the *SS Nord* Division, was not accustomed to facing such a difficult situation. The most serious shortcoming was a lack of coordination between the various units and higher headquarters. The regiment was supposed to receive fire support from the divisional artillery regiment. *SS-Nachrichten Kompanie 54* maintained telephone and radio communications up until the last minute. However, after 17:00 telephonic contact with the regiment was cut due to enemy artillery fire. *SS-Ostubaf.* Benner delayed transferring the artillery and heavy weapons units, but above all he wasted precious time in deciding whether to proceed along the Narva-Reval road or along the railway line. The order to fall back to the *Tannenbergstellung* arrived from the

Brigade headquarters via radio. However, the movement could not begin until the artillery regiment first began its move. *SS-Stubaf.* Schlüter received a separate order that directed that all of his guns were to be pulled back to the west. Several batteries of the *Nederland* artillery regiment were delayed owing to a shortage of vehicles.

SS-Stubaf. Wilhelm Schlüter.

Members of *SS-Pz.Jäg.Abt.54* taken during a moment of rest.

A soldier fires the *MG-34* from atop a *StuG III*.

A *StuG.III* attacking enemy positions, July 1944.

At 20:00, *SS-Ostubaf.* Benner called his commanders to a meeting at his command post in Narva; these included the commanders of *I./General Seyffardt, SS-Stubaf.* Karl Betzwieser, of *II./General Seyffardt, SS-Stubaf.* Helmut Breymann, of *II./de Ruyter* (*SS-Hstuf.* Frühauf), of *SS-Art.Rgt. 54* (*SS-Stubaf.* Schlüter), and *SS-Ustuf.* Philipp Römmelt, platoon leader of *1./SS-Pz.Jg.Abt. 54*. He discussed the withdrawal to the *Tannenbergstellung* with them. Around 21:00, *SS-Ustuf.* Gustav Seinfeldt, a Brigade staff officer, brought a written order authorizing the withdrawal. At 21:30, from headquarters of the 20th SS Division, the news came that the Soviets had already reached the main supply route at Olgino. At that point, *SS-Hstuf.* Frühauf received the order to protect and if possible take the Narva-Tallin highway from the enemy forces, with the support of the two assault guns under *SS-Ustuf*. Römmelt. The *Bataillon Rebane*, which was already in the area of Olgino, was to have participated in the action.

SS-Hstuf. **Carl-Heinz Frühauf.**

Waffen SS **soldiers carrying a wounded comrade to the rear.**

A *Waffen SS* **soldier with two** *MG-34.*

German grenadiers in movement, July 1944.

The men under *SS-Hstuf*. Frühauf thus began to move to the west along the highway, establishing contact with Estonian units of the *Bataillon Rebane* (II.47th SS Regiment) at Vanaküla. Following a quick counterattack the enemy units were pushed back north of Olgino. Römmelt's two assault guns played an active role in the action. While *Bataillon Rebane* remained in place to defend the road, *II./de Ruyter* continued its march to the west. Frühauf's battalion clashed with several enemy units along the main road, managing to destroy several Soviet tanks. After having deployed his men in a ditch that ran along the road, he awaited the arrival of units from *General Seyffardt*. From that time on, however, communications with Benner had broken down. Around 23:00, other Soviet forces cut the highway to Peeterristi, but were quickly thrown back by Frühauf's men. In the meantime, at 21:50 *SS-Ostubaf*. Benner had received a new radio message from Brigade headquarters which informed him that the time of the beginning of the withdrawal had been moved to 22:00. A subsequent message reported a further delay until 23:15, a delay that proved to be fatal for the regiment. Once he had received the news that the highway had been cut in several places by Soviet units, Benner decided along with his two battalion commanders to pull back along the railway line. This was a tragic choice.

A *StuG.III* and German soldiers, Summer 1944.

German soldiers cross a burning village, July 1944.

A German tracked vehicle towing a well camouflaged *Pak* gun, Summer 1944.

A tragic withdrawal

At the hour set for the withdrawal to begin, all of the component elements of *General Seyffardt* assembled at the railway station of Narva/Kreenholm, following which they began their march following the railroad tracks. At 3:30 on 26 July, the leading elements reached Soldino, with the last arriving at 5:00. According to the testimony of several veterans, once they had reached Soldino, Benner received additional bad news: the Soviets had reached the railway line and had blocked the highway at Peeterristi. The commander then decided to return to the highway and to attack the "Reds" at Peeterristi, where he expected to find other friendly forces. However he changed his mind again when some of his scouts told him that they had found an alternate route that led from Soldino to Laagna. Frühauf waited in vain at Peeterristi until 8:00 for the arrival of Benner's regiment. Around 5:30, the remnants of the *General Seyffardt* Regiment began its march towards Laagna, through a wooded and swampy area, that soon made movement of the heavy vehicles difficult. By now, it was no longer possible to turn back and the march proceeded slowly and inexorably. From the air, Soviet planes bombed the Dutch columns, bogged down in the Estonian swamps and forests, many times. Soviet artillery also began to harass Benner's column, thanks to an observation balloon that was hovering over the swamp at Körge further to the south. Around 8:00, the leading elements of the regiment reached the area south of Tuulukse. Frühauf's battalion (*II./de Ruyter*), after having waited in vain for Benner to arrive at Peeterristi, sought to find the *General Seyffardt*, but was forced to retire from the area to the west of Laagna because of strong enemy pressure. When the I Battalion of *SS-Stubaf.* Betzwieser emerged from the forest and attempted to attack Tuulukse, it found itself facing the fire of an entire Soviet infantry battalion supported by a tank unit. The regiment's anti-tank guns, which were quickly emplaced at the edge of the forest, quickly opened fire on the enemy armor, firing until the last round. During the hellish encounter four enemy tanks were knocked out, but this did not save the Dutch battalion from total annihilation, which fought doggedly to the last man, yielding only because of the strong enemy superiority.

Waffen SS anti-tank position with *StuG 40* and *Pak 38.*

A *Waffen SS* officier on a *SdKfz.251.*

SS-Rottenführer **Derk Elsko Bruins.**

When news was received of the action at Laagna, the last of the assault guns of the *Nederland* Brigade were sent to the area to try to open an escape route for the *Seyffardt* Regiment. During this attack, *SS-Rottenführer* Derk Elsko Bruins[2], a *Geschützführer* in the *1./SS-Panzerjäger-Abteilung 54*, knocked out eight enemy tanks with his *Sturmgeschütz*. On 23 August 1944, he would be awarded the Knight's Cross and would be promoted to *Oberscharführer* for having destroyed a total of 12 enemy tanks. The attack by the *Nederland* assault guns was however easily overcome by the numerical advantage held by the Soviet tanks; two vehicles, those commanded by Kuyl and Pempelt, were lost during the engagements. *II./de Ruyter* was again forced to pull back from its positions between Laagna and Repniku under the threat of a renewed enemy attack. *SS-Aufklärungs-Kompanie 54* under *SS-*

Ostuf. Erich Kuhne, which remained in place until 9:00 as a rear guard, ended up being surrounded by the Soviets on a farm near Repniku and was completely wiped out. A few survivors were taken prisoner, but nothing else was heard about them.

A *StuG III* assault gun moves across open ground.

Waffen SS mortar crew.

Waffen SS grenadiers during a withdrawal.

In the same area the tragedy of the *General Seyffardt* played itself out. After having used up all of the ammunition for the heavy weapons, *SS-Ostubaf* Benner ordered his men to destroy them to prevent the enemy from using them. At 9:07, the Regiment sent his final radio message to the Brigade headquarters: "*...We are fighting to try to open a gap through the forest south of Laagna to the west!*". Around 10:00, the *Nederland* headquarters once again tried to establish radio contact with the regiment: "*...Where are you? There are still German units in Repniku, but also enemy units, be careful!*". Having probably received this final message, *SS-Ostubaf.* Benner decided to proceed with the survivors in the direction of Repniku. As soon as he reached the vicinity of the position, after another exhausting march through the swampy forest, Benner discussed the plan of attack with Betzwieser and Breymann. *II./General Seyffardt* was to lead the attack. Its mission was to open a gap through the enemy positions to allow the rest of the units to pass through. It was a bold plan, but it did not take into account the fact that there were no longer any German forces in Repniku. The attack was kicked off at 17:30; after only a few minutes *SS-Ostubaf.* Benner was killed while leading his men in a desperate attack against the Soviet positions. Confusion and panic took hold over most of the Dutch volunteers, who ended up under a massive enemy artillery barrage, and who found themselves completely scattered. In small groups, they tried to reach friendly lines further to the west, but only a few dozen survivors were able to succeed in that desperate attempt. Among the survivors was *SS-Ustuf.* Cornelius Nieuwendijk-Hoek[3], commander of *5.Kompanie*, who was able to confirm the death of the commander, Benner, in the field. Those that did not die in the fighting ended up in the hands of the Soviets. Many of the Dutch volunteers preferred to fight to the last bullet and let themselves be killed rather than surrender to the hated Bolsheviks. According to reports by German radio intercept units, a Soviet artillery unit captured twelve German soldiers on 26 July; at 8:20 near the railway station of Auwere. Another unit reported the capture of four men of the *Seyffardt*, following a firefight that day. On 30 July, another Soviet unit captured four members of *SS-Panzer-Aufklärungs-Kompanie 54* and *SS-Pionier-Bataillon 54* who had been wandering about in the forest since 27 July. Soviet radio carried a message announcing that officers Betzweiser and Breymann had committed suicide rather than be taken prisoner.

SS-Hstuf. **Carl-Heinz Frühauf.**

Breymannn assuredly fell in combat, but with respect to Betzweiser several sources state that he was kept in a Soviet concentration camp until 1955, when he was released. At Chanelo, *SS-Hstuf.* Frühauf was able to gather together other survivors of the Dutch 48th Regiment. *SS-Hstuf.* Friedrich Tröger, formerly the commander of the *General Seyfardt Stabskompanie*, assumed command of the *Kampfgruppe* that bore his name, in which the few survivors of the regiment were gathered along with other German personnel that had belonged to *Kriegsmarine* infantry units.

Notes

[1] The platoon to which soldiers who had committed infractions against the military code were assigned, for example for having disobeyed an order, and which was often used in dangerous missions or doing heavy labor in the rear area.

[2] Derk Elsko Bruins was born on 20 March 1923 at Vlagtwedde in the province of Groningen in the Netherlands. In 1941, he enlisted as a volunteer in the *Waffen SS*.

[3] Cornelius Nieuwendijk-Hoek, born on 22.07.1919 in Batavia (Nederland). He served as *SS-Sturmman* in *the 2./SS-Flak-Abt.5*. After graduated in the *9.Kriegs-Junker-Lehrgang* in *SS-Junkerschule* Bad Tölz and promoted *Untersturmführer* on 01/09/1943, he assigned as *Chef* in the *1./Pz.Gren.Rgt.48* on July 1944.

Bibliography

M. Afiero, "*23.SS-Freiwilligen-Panzergrenadier-Division Nederland*", Ass. Culturale Ritterkreuz

M. Afiero, "*The 23rd Waffen SS Vol.Pz.Gr.Div. Nederland*", Schiffer Publishing

M. Afiero, "*Nordland*", Marvia Edizioni

J. Mabire, "*Division Nordland*", Jacques Grancher Editeur

W. Tiecke, "*Tragedy of Faithful: a history of the III. SS-Panzer Korps*", Fedorowicz Publishing

Georg Diers – (s) SS-Pz. Abt. 503 Tank Commander
by Peter Mooney

Georg (Left) as a recruit in the *Waffen-SS*.

Georg on guard duty.

Georg Diers was born on the 2nd of November 1921, on the Wiefelstede area of Germany. His father ran a farm and Georg was being taught that trade from the hands of his father, as he got older. He was a member of the *Deutsche Jungfolk* and later the *Hitler Youth*. His entry into the *Waffen-SS* began at the start of April 1940. He initially went to *SS-Regiment Germania*, but within a few months, was moved to *SS-Regiment Nordland*, located then in Klagenfurt, Austria. After some illness suffered from an attempt to learn mountain warfare, he spent time with the Replacement Battalion for *Totenkopf* in April 1941. He was then back with *Nordland* from September 1941. His unit was located in Russia then, so Georg made the journey south-eastwards; reaching his destination in November. His first taste of the USSR was on the Mius front and he would get to know that area for the next eight months. In that time, he saw many of his Kameraden become casualties, due to the extreme cold prevailing then. He engaged in limited actions with the enemy during his first winter battles in the Soviet Union. It was during those skirmishes that he also witnessed the first combat deaths and injuries to his friends, as well as the Soviet enemy. Many of his Kameraden soon resided in the Uspenskaya cemetery, a well-known 'landmark' for the men of *SS-Division Wiking*. As the winter weather passed and Spring arrived, the skirmishes increased, as did the number of dead and wounded. The enemy activity increased notably, as the first anniversary of the German invasion of Soviet Russia arrived. Georg and his Kameraden moved from that area around mid-July 1942. They moved on into the Caucasus region to begin a lengthy operation in that southern-most region of the USSR. It was also in July that Diers began training on the *PaK 36* anti-tank gun. This 'anti-tank' role would take him on a career path that would lead to Berlin in April 1945, but a few more notable items to cover first!

K98 Rifle shooting practice.

Following almost 2-weeks of gun training, they made their moves towards Rostov. (Rostov on Don was first attacked by the *Waffen-SS* in the previous winter, with Heinrich Springer being awarded the Knight's Cross for his actions there). For Georg, that significant location was secured by Kameraden from *Wiking*, ahead of his own advance. (At least 2 *Wiking* soldiers got their Knight's Cross for their actions there in July 1942). Over the closing days of July 1942 and the first week of August, Georg helped to secure the Maikop area. As he advanced deeper southwards, the terrain became more and more mountainous. His earlier training attempts would have served him well here and looks like his 'unsuitability' for mountain warfare was a mute point. For the remainder of August 1942, he moved to the southeast. Towards the

Uspenskaja cemetery in the USSR.

end of September, they were advancing on Grosny, around 500 miles from Rostov. It was during that fighting that Georg Diers was badly wounded and had to be evacuated. Initially flown out by Ju 52, he went first to Poland, but was then moved to Vienna. His wound was to his arm and Georg underwent some intense 'discussions' with the Doctors, as well as some very intense pain, as he fought to get over the effects of his severe wound. As he was recovering, one of his close friends kept him up to date with life at the front line, via feldpost. One notable letter covered a 25-day period for the men left at the front and within the unit that Georg had been a part off, 26 soldiers were killed and 37 wounded. Those casualty figures give an insight into the 'challenges' that the men at the frontline, in southeast Russia, faced in the closing weeks of 1942. Georg's return to active duty, which literally hung in the balance as 1942 ended, finally resumed in mid-1943.

PaK 36 training for Georg and his Kameraden.

Georg Diers after his promotion to *SS-Unterscharführer.*

He once again arrived at *Nordland* and the next phase of his career got underway. Georg was holding *SS-Unterscharfuhrer* rank by then. He started training on tanks, initially in Germany, but then continued that in Croatia – where *Nordland* were located in the second half of 1943. Part of Georg's experiences there included the disarming of the Italian troops positioned in Croatia, as well as anti-Partisan fighting, using captured Italian tanks, which were small, but suitable for this region. In November 1943, Georg was moved to the newly created *(schwere) SS-Panzer Abteilung 103*. For his training on the heavy tanks, he was sent back to northern Germany and trained on into the early part of 1944. January and February seen him locate to Holland for further training, before following that with a two-month stint at Paederborn. Their training was hampered by the supply of Tiger Is, which was slow and limited.

Tiger I training, 18th August 1944.

He returned to Holland and was there when the Allied invasion got underway. For Georg, despite the concerns about this 'new' enemy threat, he had the joy of being granted home-leave to get married. In August 1944, their Tiger Is were used to help the men undergo intensive training in Holland, on this formidable fighting vehicle. It was during this heavy tank training that Georg forged close friendships with some of his Kameraden; some of which would be part of his crew until the end of the conflict (and beyond). They moved back to Germany in September and then in October, they began to take delivery of Tiger IIs. They seen out the rest of 1944 there and also seen the change in their name to the *(schwere) SS-Panzer Abteilung 503*. In late-January 1945, this formation was loaded onto trains and sent to Pomerania, northeast of Berlin, to defend that area against the onslaught of the advancing Russians. In the opening days of February 1945, fighting took place around Arnswalde, where Georg and his tank helped to free thousands of civilians from a Soviet encircling ring. In the second half of that month, the westwards movements seen Georg in Danzig and then Gollnow. March seen his 'advance' go through Altdamm and Prenzlau. April seen them move closer and closer to Berlin. Angermunde and Grunow were locations he moved through. In the third week of that month, he was part of a small tank troop that engaged a large column of Russian tanks. They decimated that forces within a short timeframe, estimations are that over 25% of the enemy forces were destroyed, with zero losses to the 4 tanks that Georg formed part of. Post-war discussions in the very area of this fight, stated the recovery and burial of around 1,000 Soviet troops.

SS-Uscha. **Georg Diers.**

In the closing part of April 1945, Georg was located around Honow, around 50 miles southwest of Angermunde. On the 21st of April, Georg was located in Tempelhof, whilst his tank was undergoing some repairs in a nearby workshop. Once his tank was repaired, the advance of the Soviets had reached the outskirts of the capital. Georg's tank was one of 6 Tiger II tanks from *(s) SS-Pz.Abt. 503* located in Berlin from that time, and they therefore formed a notable portion of the mobile defences against the final fight for Berlin. Over the closing days of April 1945, defensive fighting took place for Georg and his tank around Neukolln and Hasenheide, Hermannplatz and Potsdamer Platz. During those interesting few days, Georg almost found himself captured by the Soviet troops, after he became separated from his tank / crew. They helped to inflict losses on the advancing and seemingly inexhaustable numbers of Soviet tanks and troops. On the final day of April 1945, he was ordered to the Reichstag. It was there that Georg and his crew engaged and destroyed a force of 30 *T-34* Soviet tanks, who were located near the Brandenburg Gate. He then helped to defend the immediate area south of the *Reichstag*, down to the Kroll Opera House; that was in the opening day of May. His following actions also involved fighting enemy tanks around the opera house, then also firing upon the Brandenburg Gate, to help 'free-it' of the enemy.

Heinz Turk's tank at the Potsdammer railway station.

SS-Oscha. Heinz Turk.

SS-Brigadeführer Wilhelm Mohnke, awarded Georg his First Class Iron Cross.

He moved back to the *Reichstag*. As that day unfolded, he was ordered to the Reich's Chancellery and there, was ordered to take part in the planned breakout. It was during that visit, that Georg was informed about the death of Adolf Hitler. The site of the planned breakout for Georg, and the remaining high dignitaries of the Third Reich, was to be the Weidendammer Bridge. That visit to the Reich's Chancellery brought Georg in contact with many of the top Generals and Politicians of that era and it must have been an unusual occurrence for a 'lowly' soldier of the *Waffen-SS*? Another notable memory for him, as part of that visit, was the awarding of the First Class Iron Cross, from the hands of *SS-Brigadefuhrer* Wilhelm Mohnke. In the closing hours of the 2nd of May 1945, Georg located himself at that bridge and awaited the final order to move across it. As he did so, more and more soldiers and civilians arrived in the night. The attempt itself took place just after midnight and although Georg made it through with his tank, it was badly shot up and his passengers on the back were cut to pieces by the enemy fire pouring down upon them.

That was the fate for most of the soldiers and civilians who followed behind in lighter armoured and non-armoured vehicles. Georg continued to advance through the warren of streets on the other side of the river, guided by another soldier. It was around Schonhauser Allee that they stopped and after much consultation with Monhke and General Barenfanger, the decision was made to destroy the tank and make the rest of the journey on foot. That journey was done with small groups of survivors and for Georg, they moved to the north. For Georg, his journey and freedom came to an end at Havelberg, around 75 miles northwest of the Weidendammer bridge. He reached that location in mid-May 1945 and remained there until mid-June. On the 18th of June, he placed his trust in a local community leader; that leader betrayed him and he was taken prisoner by Soviet troops.

Georg returns to the Wiedendammer bridge - the scene of the May 1945 breakout from the Berlin inner ring.

After a short trial, he was sentenced to death, due to being a soldier from the *Waffen-SS*. Bluff and luck played their part and he managed to evade that outcome. He did however, begin a five-year spell in Soviet prison camps; that included a location in Moscow. Georg Dier's return to civilian life took place during Christmas 1949. Following that, Georg set about forging a life for himself and his family. He established a very successful meat processing Company and ran that until the early 1980s, when he sold it and retired. Georg Diers was active in the various *Waffen-SS* veteran associations and attended many of their Treffens. It was at one of those where I first met him and spoke to him.

Georg Diers retained a diary for most of his military service and the contents helped to form the basis of the German-language book, *'Tiger in Berlin: Ein Soldat der Waffen-SS berichtet'*, published by Am Wall Publishing in 2016. The English-language version is printed by Loyalty and Honour Publishing under the title, *'For the Defence of Berlin'*. That expanded version of the original German-language book comes with the short recollections of Oskar Schafer and also the written Berlin recollections of Henri Fenet.

Please contact: contactus@lahpublishing.com for details of how to obtain your own copy.

The Albanian element of Waffen-SS from Bosnian "Handschar" to Albanian "Skanderbeg" division

by Dmitry Frolov - Part I

Reichsführer-SS **Heinrich Himmler speaking with** *Waffen-SS* **volunteers in Sennheim.**

The European way of Waffen-SS

A study of relations between various nations during the Second World War gives Nazi Germany a special place in historical science. A special part here was played by the rule of the ethnic exclusiveness of Nazi doctrine, which put certain obstacles to cooperation of its forces with peoples of countries under Reich control. This "ethnic barrier" was felt especially by representatives of so-called "non-Germanic" peoples (the French, Spanish, Walloons, etc.). While volunteers from Scandinavian countries (Norway, Denmark, Finland) and Western Europe (Holland and Flemish region of Belgium) were a part of the "elite" troops of *Waffen-SS* from the beginning of World War II, residents of Eastern and South-Eastern Europe had no opportunity to join those units.

German recruitment campaign for the volunteers of the Bosnia-Herzegovina.

They started military service in local *Wehrmacht* troops. Thus, the question of their location didn't arise in the racial policy of Nazism while Germany was enjoying its early victories. What forced the Reich Command review their attitude were growing losses combined with the necessity to control previously-conquered territories. The following changes primarily dealt with military troops of the Nazi party – *Waffen-SS*, which were no longer ready to follow the principles of selection, based on a policy of racial purity. Absence of "Germanic" volunteers to fulfil military reserve requirements opened the door to peoples of South-Eastern Europe to join the *Waffen-SS*. A recruitment campaign of March, 1942 among ethnic Germans of Croatia and Serbia was the first step to changing the SS primary, but no longer up-to-date priorities. Soon after that the need to fight against the communist guerrilla movement of J.Broz (Tito) in the Independent State of Croatia (ISC) made the SS-leaders broaden their capabilities and recruit the Muslims of Bosnia and Herzegovina, which was part of Croatia at that moment, to their ranks.

Zagreb 1943, first Bosnian volunteers for the *Handschar* Division.   *Waffen SS* **Volunteer.**

...They fight with us for Europe (from German magazine, *Kolnische Illustrierte Zeitung*).

That was primarily related to active Nazi propaganda of the "New Europe" idea, which replaced the concept of European peoples' "crusade" against Bolshevism. Thus, the SS-reinforcement was expressed by both their successful rivalry with the *Wehrmacht* in hiring potential recruits and political claims of their leader – *Reichsführer-SS* Heinrich Himmler. A proper example of stating the new Nazi propaganda-concept is Himmler's speech, presented at the session of racial policy service meeting on January 28, 1944: *"Our time does rush forward and we have a new – European – stage of development. New European peoples are here: the Latvians, Estonians, Galicians, Bosnians, Croatians and Albanians, old and new peoples of the Reich, living in Europe"*. The initiative of Himmler and his ally – chief of the SS Main Office *SS-Obergruppenführer* Gottlob Berger – to create the 13th Waffen Mountain Division of the SS *"Handschar"*, consisting of Bosnian Muslims, was approved on February 10, 1943. This became the starting point in the process of expansive *Waffen-SS* development and their transformation to national combat units. Despite Himmler's priority to recruit the Muslims of Bosnia and Herzegovina into the new combat force, the division was formed by volunteers, who had no relation to Croatia. These were mostly Albanian residents of the Sandzak and Kosovo together with a few Bulgarian Muslims, who possibly joined the division much later.

Himmler and Berger during an inspection to a SS unit.

Sandjak militiamen, 1944.

SS-Standartenführer **Karl von Krempler, Senior *Führer* of SS and police in Sandzak, Spring 1944.**

Italian sources, emphasizing plans of Germany to organize recruitment among the "Muslim elements" at the end of 1942, mentioned the plans to recruit Albanian citizens of the Sandzak (Sandjak). The first Albanian volunteers were enlisted to *Waffen-SS* from the Sandzak in March, 1943. Just like it was with the Muslim population of Bosnia, control of the recruitment process was the responsibility of *SS-Obersturmführer* Karl von Krempler – an officer of Croatian SS-Volunteer Division Control Headquarters (future *"Handschar"*), which was being organized in Zagreb. On April 29, 1943 *SS-Gruppenführer* and Lieutenant-General Artur Phleps reported to *SS-Reichsführer* Himmler of recruiting to the *Waffen-SS* of at least 8-10 thousand Muslim volunteers from the Sandzak. In Spring, 1943 the Albanians together with Bosnian volunteers were sent to southern France – the cities of Le Puy and Villefranche-de-Rouergue - for military education. *SS-Obergruppenführer* Gottlob Berger highly evaluated the Albanians' readiness to fight for SS and underlined their typical courage and principles.

The Mufti of Jerusalem visits the *Handschar* Division.

Amin al Husseini and Adolf Hitler, Berlin 1943.

The attitude of the chief of the SS Main Office met Himmler's concept in necessity to find a basis in the "special consciousness" of the Albanians, who hated the Serbians, constituting the major part of guerila troops of Josif Broz (Tito). Thus they could be involved in a war against guerrillas on the side of Germany.

Across cultures: the Albanian element of "Handschar" Division

While preparing the Bosnian SS-Division for war against guerrillas in Bosnia, SS-leaders considered *"Handschar"*, which was essentially Muslim, to be a combat force with propaganda meaning. The VI Department, responsible for organizing ideologically-worldview work within the division, pointed out the connection of *"Handschar"* with Albanian Muslims, considering the Muslim SS-Division to be a step on the way to creating a similar unit in Albania. This was supported by the image of Albania as of territory – part of a *"Muslim SS-basis"* for further SS-*"Muslim experiment"*. The visit of the Grand Mufti of Jerusalem to Bosnia had its role, too, since his arrival and care for coreligionists impressed the representatives of Albanian Muslims greatly. Recruitment of the Albanians to *"Handschar"* continued until the capitulation of Italy in autumn, 1943 and following re-organization of the Albanian state. The Italians' withdrawal from the war forced the Germans to organize disarmament of parts of the Italian army and take the territories, previously-occupied by them. In Albania the

Wehrmacht was represented by troops of *100.Jäger-Division* with approximately 1000 men. Just before the capitulation of Italy parts of the German army seized the country's airports and the port of Durres. Final occupation of Albania was completed by September 9, 1943 by troops of the *2.Panzer-Armee*, which was in the second echelon. Just as had happened in Bosnia, the entrance of *Wehrmacht* into Albanian cities caused no problems from local citizens. A vital role here was played by the principles of "collective memory". Arrival of the Germans declared freedom from Bolshevism and from the Anglo-Saxon threat.

German soldiers in Albania, September 1943.

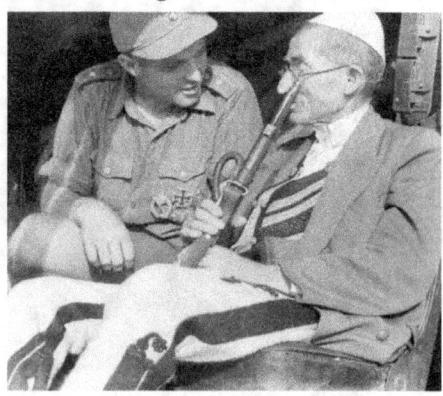

German soldier talking to an Albanian.

Albanian volunteers, Autumn 1943.

Albanian fighting against guerillas.

The *Wehrmacht* also struck a sympathetic note, as both the Albanians and the Bosnians had good memories of the Austro-Hungarian Army. Local citizens associated it with ground forces and *Waffen-SS*. Arrival of SS-recruitment teams to Albania, which was different from the agreement of recruiting in Bosnian territories only, caused protests by Siegfried Kasche. He was an ambassador of the Reich in the ISC and characterized these actions of the SS as the "worst impression", provided on the Croatian side. Just as before, the Ministry of Foreign Affairs was in the way of the *Waffen-SS* – it was forced to follow the "neutral" policy considering the existing Albanian government. First of all, it was due to the SS overriding the competence of the Ministry concerning international matters and different opinions of departments on the place of Bosnian Muslims in the Reich's policy. A ministry representative, Eberhard von Thadden, declared the necessity to avoid transfer of already-recruited Albanians across the borders of Albania. He also considered it a must that they came under command of the Albanian Ministry of Internal Affairs. By autumn, 1943, *SS-Obergruppenführer* Berger reported that of 6000 Albanians (citizens of Serbia) recruited by the *Wehrmacht* High Command (*Oberkommando der Wehrmacht*). 2/3 were from Sandzak and 1/3 from Kosovo, with no uniforms and equipped with primarily Italian weapons. Gottlob Berger ordered the Senior *SS-Führers* and police to immediately list these Albanian volunteers since there was danger of their recruitment by English agents who, as he said, "had a lot of gold".

After Italy's surrender, the *Albanian-Muslim volunteer SS-Legion*, was amply armed with Italian weapons supplied to them by the German (*Bundesarchiv*).

A Moslem fighter of the *Sandjak Militia*, 1943.

The bulk of these volunteers were to be used to complete another unit of the SS and police of Balkans – the "Albanian-Muslim volunteer SS-Legion". This four-squadron unit, also known as "Volunteer Legion of Krempler", took part in fighting against guerillas near Sandzak and, as Wolfgang Vopersal believes, was partly integrated into the "*Handschar*" SS-Division. The Reich ambassador in Albania, Hermann Neubacher, managed to persuade Himmler to stop recruitment of the Albanians into the *Waffen-SS*. This was achieved with the assistance of the Chief of Security Police and SD (security service of *SS-Reichsführer*), *SS-Obergruppenführer* and police General Ernst Kaltenbrunner. Gottlob Berger stated that

Himmler's ban reflected on *Waffen-SS* plans on forming battalions in Albania, while WHC (*Wehrmacht* High Command) ignored any limits and recruited the Albanians for their own use and, competing with the SS, formed five battalions with 4800 people. Neubacher recalled: *"When I started to work in Albania, followers of Muslim SS-Division "Handschar", organized in Bosnia, arrived in Kosovo. With the help of Kaltebrunner I managed to persuade Himmler give up the idea of recruiting the Albanians from Kosovo for forming the SS-Division, as it had been done previously in Bosnia. This confronts our neutral policy concerning Albania".*

Hermann Neubacher.

Sandjak militiamen: note the young age of volunteers.

Albanian *Handschar* battalion on the move, 1944.

Except for protest against actions of SS-recruitment teams, Neubacher required pullout of Albanian SS-members, recruited to the Division, and their return to Albania. At the same time the ambassador stated that Himmler, relying on traditions of elite Bosnian troops of the Austro-Hungarian Empire, reached his goal to organize further recruitment of Muslim citizens of the region into the *Waffen-SS*. Despite serious support of Neubacher by Minister of Internal Affairs Joachim Ribbentrop, Berger managed to stop the pullout of already-recruited Albanian SS-members by referring to needed reinforcement of the Bosnian SS-Division and a few-weeks-delay in its forming, caused by the removal of

opinion, *"formal details played a vital role for strengthening the Division"*. It also became clear that the Bosnians and Albanians could not reach a mutual understanding, which led to altercations in the barracks, often with use of knives.

Unteroffizier of Albanian battalion Rudolf Sommerer (*George Lepre Collection*).

Himmler with the commander of the *Handschar* Division, *SS-Brigdf*. Sauberzweig.

SS-Ogruf. Artur Phleps (*Andrey Zubkov Collection*).

As for the moral image of the Albanians, German commanders believed it was similar to that of the Bosnians – far from the proper image of a German SS-soldier. The disdainful attitude of German commanders towards Muslim soldiers together with low service conditions (due to food-supplies problems) and hard training became one of the reasons that led to a mutiny among Muslim SS-soldiers of 13th SS-Engineer Battalion in the French city of Villefranche-de-Rouergue on September 17, 1943. Secretary of the Croatian embassy in Berlin Milan Blazekovic noted, that after repressing the mutiny, the Germans sent a few hundred Bosnian Muslims and the Albanians to concentration camps, where the latter faced regular humiliation from the SS. All of them were mainly unserviceable for the army, still willing to fight but not work. In his letter to Vopersal, Blazekovic said that the Muslims in captivity were looking for protection from the Croatian embassy in Berlin. Still, attempts of the Croatians to influence the Germans were useless, especially since the camp commandant forbid any contacts between the camp and the embassy. A member of the resistance movement, professor Rudi Supek from Zagreb, recalled that after Italy surrendered in September, 1943, many Yugoslavs arrived at the Buchenwald concentration camp. Among them, there were a few sets of prisoners, who called themselves Croatians and Muslims. As Supek said, they also became an object for victimization by the Germans. Division Command understood the necessity to improve the morale of Muslim soldiers, which is why they raised the question of improving food supplies (extra provision of flour, sugar, butter and fish) at the summit level.

The Grand Mufti and *SS-Brigdf*. Sauberzweig, Autumn 1943.

***SS-Brigdf*. Sauberzweig.**

SS-Obf. **Sauberzweig at a shooting range with his soldiers during their formation and training in southern France, summer of 1943.**

SS-Brigadeführer Karl Sauberzweig managed to get Hitler's approval, who was assured of the Muslim volunteers' "loyalty, obedience and eagerness" – thus he expected to maintain support of SS-Muslims. As seen by *SS-Brigadeführer* Karl Sauberzweig the following entrance of 13th Waffen Mountain Division of the SS into Bosnia showed that the Albanians overcame some national-cultural borders. At the moment the Division reached Bosnian border, Sauberzweig gave the Albanian soldiers of "*Handschar*" a fatherlike speech: "*We have arrived here, to the border of Bosnia, and in a few days, as soon as we are altogether, we will begin our march home. For you, my dear Albanians, this march is a way home. As soon as you, dear Albanians, cross the Bosnian border, you will enter the society of the Muslims, which is like a bridge between the Sava and your mountains. [...] Hail Homeland, from Bosnia to Albania!*"

Pro-German ceremony, Pec 1944.

We should point out that the following reassignment of the Albanian battalion, pulled out of *"Handschar"* for creating the Albanian SS-Division required its full reorganization, as stated by Sauberzweig. As a result the Division Commander gave credit for combat qualities of an Albanian SS-soldier, defining the connection with the Albanian battalion, for which he had special feelings: *"I must point out the special courage of the Albanians who, surrounded and outnumbered by the enemy, continued fighting and showed uncommon bravery. They are the messengers of their country, a connection which we were looking for and will definitely find"*. As stated by Commander of V Mountain Corps of the SS, *SS-Obergruppenführer* Phleps, the Albanian battalion of the Bosnian SS-Division was the best in the division and proved itself to be reliable at fighting in difficult-to-access mountain regions of Bosnia. A researcher of the Dublin Centre for War Studies, Franziska Zaugg, points out that the devotion of the Albanian battalion of SS-Division *"Handschar"* to its commander *SS-Brigadeführer* Sauberzweig caused further problems when subordinating the battalion to the future Albanian SS-Division– this caused "a lot of sorrow" among the Albanians, as Berger said. Knowing how to fight in combat conditions and considered one of the most battleworthy elements of the *"Handschar"* Division, the Albanian battalion, being better prepared ideologically and militarily, was to become an example for those Albanians, who were to start their military service as part of the *Waffen-SS*. Still, the initiative of creating the new Muslim SS-Division dictated other terms…

Reference List

1) Archive materials

National Archives of the United States. Washington D.C. (NARA); T-175, Roll 70, 94; T-120, Roll 1757.
Bundesarchiv-Militärarchiv. N 756. Sammlung Vopersal, zur Geschichte der Waffen-SS (BA-MA. N 756. Sign. 169a, 168b, 182b).

2) Studies

Zaugg F. «*Perfekte Krieger*»? Die deutsche Wahrnehmung muslimischer Albaner in der Waffen-SS zwischen 1943 und 1945 // Wegner/Schulte/Lieb (Hg.), Die Waffen-SS. Neue Forschungen.

Zaugg F. Albanische Muslime in der Waffen-SS. Von «Grossalbanien« zur division «Skanderbeg». Ferdinand Schöningh. Paderborn. 2016. 346 s.

Littlejohn D. Foreign Legions of the Third Reich.Vol.3. R James Bender Pub. 384 p.

Vopersal W. «Scanderbeg». Geschichte der 21.Waffen-Gebirgs Division der SS «Scanderbeg», unpublished manuscript.

Lukać D. Treći Rajh I zemlje jugoistoćne Evrope. Treći deo. Vojnoizdavački i novinski centar — Beograd. Beograd, 1987. 870 s.

Krizman B. Pavelić izmedu Hitlera i Mussolinija. Globus / Zagreb. 1980. 618 s.

Nojbaher H. Specijalni zadatak Balkan. Javno preduzeće Službeni list SCG Beograd. Beograd. 2004. 204 s.

Sulejmanpasic Z. 13. SS Divizija «Handzar». Istine i laži. Zagreb: Kulturno društvo Bošnjaka Hrvatske Preporod, 2000. 432 s.

The Leibstandarte with Army Group North
by Daniel Fanni

Leibstandarte **soldiers on the Eastern front.**

December 1941. The mighty German juggernaut has finally expended itself from its summer rampage. Bled dry from continuous attrition and on the limit of its overextended supply lines it cannot move further. Worse, the Red Army, against all hopes is not only far from exhausted but also starts to strike back hard along the frontlines. One of the first to taste this envigored Soviet might is *Generalfeldmarschall* von Kleist's 1st Panzer Army in southern Ukraine. Having just reached and taken in hard combat the city of Rostov-on-Don, a deep thrust into her exposed northern flank by the 37th Soviet Army in November precipitated the first German retreat of the campaign. Having to relinquish Rostov, the whole German front was forced to retrace its steps 60 to 80kms west, all the way back to the Mius River. One of the units taking Rostov was *SS-Gruppenführer* Josef "Sepp" Dietrich's *Leibstandarte SS 'Adolf Hitler'*. A unit which, although already being called a Division, was little more than a reinforced Brigade at this point and a heavily depleted one at that, after the non-stop drive across the Ukraine. It had taken part in most of the big engagements that characterized, *Barbarossa* in

'*Heeresgruppe Süd*' during the past six months; Kiev, Uman pocket, Kherson, Crimean isthmus, Mariupol, Taganrog and finally Rostov. Now left to entrench, as good as they could, behind the Mius Rriver at Sambek, north of Taganrog, the unit was in dire need of replacements to make up for the grievous losses. Plans were then set in motion back in Berlin precisely for these circumstances. At the *Leibstandarte's* barracks at Lichterfelde, the *V./Wachbataillon* (Guard Battalion) of the *LSSAH* was fulfilling the duties for which the very *Standarte* had been originally formed.

Berlin Lichterfelde *Leibstandarte* barracks where the *Wachbattalion* was quartered.

The *Wachbattalion* performing its representative duties through the streets of Berlin.

Designed to act as a fanatically loyal guard unit for the *Führer* himself they were tasked with guarding Hitler at the Reich Chancellery, important official buildings, the Berghoff, and also to act in protocolary events and public gatherings. Since the outbreak of war, it had become a good place where freshly recovering wounded personnel and others newly transferred to the unit would await their assignments. The Guard shared the barracks now with the *Ersatz und Ausbildungs Battalion 1* (Replacement and Training Battalion) which was tasked with providing freshly trained recruits for the frontline units of the LSSAH. It was designated the Fifth *Wachbataillon* because the other previous four infantry battalions of the *Leibstandarte* were already on the front. Following older, pre-Barbarossa plans to finally upgrade the *Leibstandarte*, at the front, to a full division, and considering its severe manpower shortages, the *V./LSSAH* was sent in December 1941 to the troop training grounds of Wildflecken in Bavaria to make the unit combat ready. On a later date, the actual 'Training and Replacement Battalion' would also leave for field training to the Sennelager training camp, by Paderborn, and should later join the Division in Russia. This would bring the *Leibstandarte* up to a total of six infantry battalions, making a two motorized infantry regiment unit as had been originally planned along with the rest of the foreseen expansion of the LSSAH into a full division.

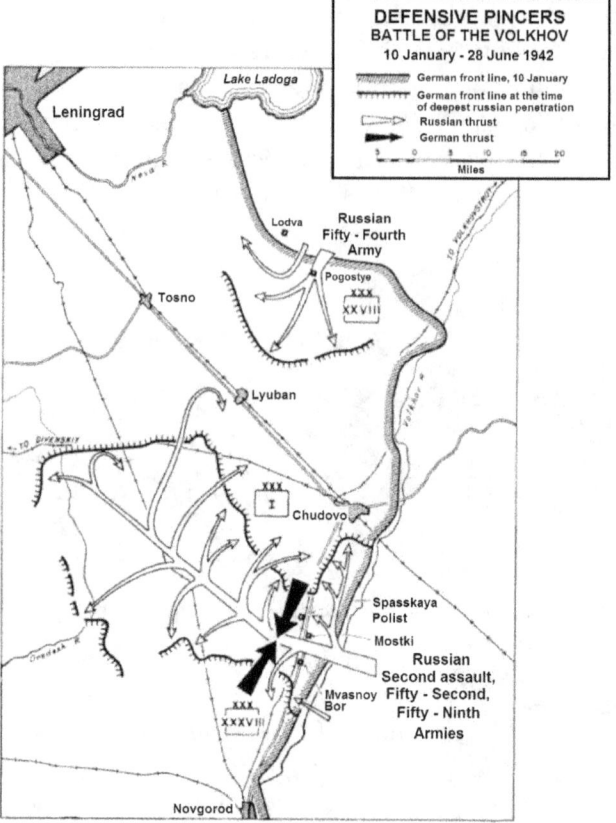

DEFENSIVE PINCERS
BATTLE OF THE VOLKHOV
10 January - 28 June 1942

German front line, 10 January
German front line at the time
of deepest russian penetration
Russian thrust
German thrust

Miles

Map showing the Soviet *Lyuban Offensive Operation* between January to May 1942, that brought about the urgent transfer of the *V./LSSAH* to the Army Group North.

German *MG-34* machine-gun position located on the edge of a village on the Volkhov front during the winter of 1941-42.

Lyuban Operation

However, conditions at the front would not allow for all this to come to fruition as planned. Along with several other major Soviet offensives that early January in 1942, STAVKA launched the Lyuban Operation. A very optimistic attack by the 'Volkhov Front' to cut through the feeble German defenses along the frozen Volkhov River, thrust deep into *'Army Group North's'* hinterland with the object of cutting through the communications zone of the 18th Army and then moving to the north in the direction of Leningrad. As the situation worsened, *'Army Group North'* tried desperately to contain this dangerous offensive by throwing in its way and on its flanks a hodge-podge of units gathered. At first these would be mere battalions freed from various divisions. These emergency actions slowed the breakthrough down, especially at its flanks near the Volkhov River. The Soviet offensive, while stalled trying to widen the initial breakthrough area, managed to reach a 75-kilometer depth before sufficient German reinforcements were able to completely halt any further advance and then started counterattacking. It soon became clear that more resources were desperately needed to face down this menace. Still unrelated to this situation (at that time) the V./LSSAH was hurriedly recalled from the Wildflecken training grounds to Berlin at the end of January and lavishly equipped for winter warfare, preparing the unit to be sent to the Eastern Front. On the 17th of February, Franz Halder, chief of the *Oberkommando des Heeres* staff, wrote in his diary; *"In conference about situation in the North, the Führer promised to send his resources to help. Result: 337 transport planes made available by 18/2. In addition, five police Battalions, the Norwegian Legion (SS) and one Battalion of the LAH"*. The V./LSSAH would be thus sent as reinforcement to 'Army Group North' and for that it was quickly readied.

SS-Sturmbannführer **Hugo Kraas, just promoted, with his Knights Cross he won leading the same Battalion (at that time** I./SS-Panzer-Grenadier Regiment 2) **during the fighting around Kharkov in the spring of 1943.**

Hugo Kraas

The new commander of this Battalion was *SS-Hauptsturmführer* Hugo Kraas who was just returning to service having been wounded in December while serving with the *LSSAH* along the Mius River. Hugo Kraas had joined the *SS-Verfügungstruppe* in 1935 as a member of the *Standarte "Germania"*. Later in 1938 he attended the *SS-Junkerschule Braunschweig* and successfully graduated second in his class as an *SS-Untersturmführer*. Posted to the *Leibstandarte* as *Zugführer*/platoon leader in the *Panzerjäger*/Antitank Company he transferred after Poland, in October, he along with his former Commander and to be mentor, *SS-Hauptsturmführer* Kurt Meyer "Panzermeyer" to the *Krad-Schützenkompanie* (motorcyclists) of the unit. He fought with them in the French, Balkan and Barbarossa Campaigns, rising to lead the 2nd Company in the fast-growing *Aufklärungs-Abteilung* (Recon Battalion) and becoming second in command to Meyer. With the latter's illness in October 1941, he eventually led the unit until Meyer's return. For his deeds during the conquest of Mariupol, Taganrog and Rostov, he was awarded the DKiG (German Cross in Gold). In Berlin-Lichterfelde, Kraas met his new company commanders, 1. *Komp. Ostuf.* Günther Hausdorf, who had joined the *LSSAH* in the newly raised *IV. Battalion* just before Barbarossa and had returned to the *Wachbataillon,* like Kraas, after being wounded on the Eastern Front. 2. *Komp. Ostuf.* Hans Becker, a very capable officer who had been part of the *LAH* since before the war, had become an officer in the *I./LAH* in 1939 and eventually rose to be Battalion commander. 3. *Komp. Hstuf.* Beutler who had been adjutant with the *II./LAH* before this transfer and would eventually become IIa (Adjudant) taking care of the personnel group (rosters, rolls, punishments, promotions, etc.) of the Divisional HQ of the *LSSAH in* June 1944. 4. (MG) *Komp. Ostuf.* Waldow and 5. (*Schw.* or Heavy weapons and Pioneers) *Komp. Hstuf.* Kaschula, who would end up leading the *VII./LSSAH Wachbataillon* in early 1943.

Ju-52 **Transport plane as used to transfer the Battalion from Berlin to the aerodromes of Ssiwerskaja and Krassnogwardeisk south of Leningrad.**

German soldiers in march, Winter 1941/42.

Leningrad front

The battalion was generously equipped with 78 brand new prototypes of the soon to-be infamous MG 42. They were instructed to prepare to be transferred to the front in the transport planes as promised by Hitler. Starting on February 22nd the first flights took off from Staaken airfield at Berlin via Königsberg and Riga to the aerodromes of Ssiwerskaja and Krassnogwardeisk south of Leningrad. Due to encountered bad weather plus the loading restrictions of only 12 fully equipped men per flight in the trusty JU-52s and JU-90s, it would take until the 28th of February for all men to arrive at their destination. Arriving already on the 25th, Kraas and his staff drove during the morning to the Headquarters of the *L. Armee Korp* at Krassnogwardeisk to receive their orders from *Generalleutnant* Kleffel. On that evening they were sent to interview with *Generalmajor* Altrichter of the *58. Infanterie-division*. To their dismay they discovered that had been assigned to be part of a newly thrown together *Kampfgruppe* which was to cover the western siege lines around Leningrad right to the coast of the Gulf of Finland. This was to enable the currently deployed *58. Infanterie-division* to be freed in order to help stop and contain the Soviet 2nd Shock Army which, at this point was still advancing from its Volkhov breakthrough. On February 26th Kraas and his staff went to visit the *154. Infanterie-Regiment* on the *58. Infanterie-division* positions, whose sector the *Wachbattalion* was to take over as ordered. There they learned the composition of the newly arriving *Kampfgruppe* which they would be part of. They found it contained all units Hitler had promised *'Army Group North'* as noted in Halder's diary entry. There would be the green Norwegian SS Legion, the five Police Battalions which had been doing garrison duty until then in Poland, and a severely depleted 320. *Infanterie-Regiment* that was part of the 212. *Infanterie-Division* that was guarding the nearby Oranienbaum pocket's lines. They were to be equipped with the heavy equipment of the 58th Infantry Division which would be left behind in their hurried transfer to the Volkhov front.

Left Photo: *SS-Obergruppenführer* **Friedrich Jeckeln, the controversial man who would lead the Kampfgruppe under his name covering the western siegeworks around Leningrad while other units there were sent to contain and destroy General Vlassov's 2nd Shock Army at the Volkhov. Right Photo: visit by General Lindemann, commander of the 50th Army Korps to the trenches of** *Kampfgruppe Jeckeln.*

Church of "Dreiecksdorf" just south of Urizk and rally point of the battalion before getting deployed into line.

The Headquarters for the *Kampfgruppe* was to be provided by the—nearby *Infanterie-Regiment* 409 of the 122. *Infanterie-Division*. To top it all off they also learned that the *Kampfgruppe* would be led *by SS-Obergruppenführer* and General of the Police Friedrich Jeckeln. Friedrich Jeckeln had been a World War I artillery officer and member of the NSDAP since 1929. He had been active with the early SS and had overseen the gradual take over by them of the regional police units. In 1936, he commanded already all the western German police forces. With the start of the war, he had commanded a battalion in the 2nd Regiment of the *Totenkopf Division* and fought in the French Campaign. After the start of

Barbarossa, he was transferred as *Höherer SS und Polizeiführer* (Higher SS and Police Leader) behind the advancing front, first to the Ukraine and later to the Baltic region, where he actively partook in anti-Partisan actions and bloody repressions to the point he even got reprimanded by Himmler himself for his methods. He eventually got executed by the Soviets for war crimes in 1946. This man was to lead the *'Kampfgruppe Jeckeln'*.

Left Photo: the school building in Urizk that served as the battalion Headquarters.
Right Photo: *SS-Hstuf*. Fritz Beutler, Commander of the 3rd Company in the Battalion.

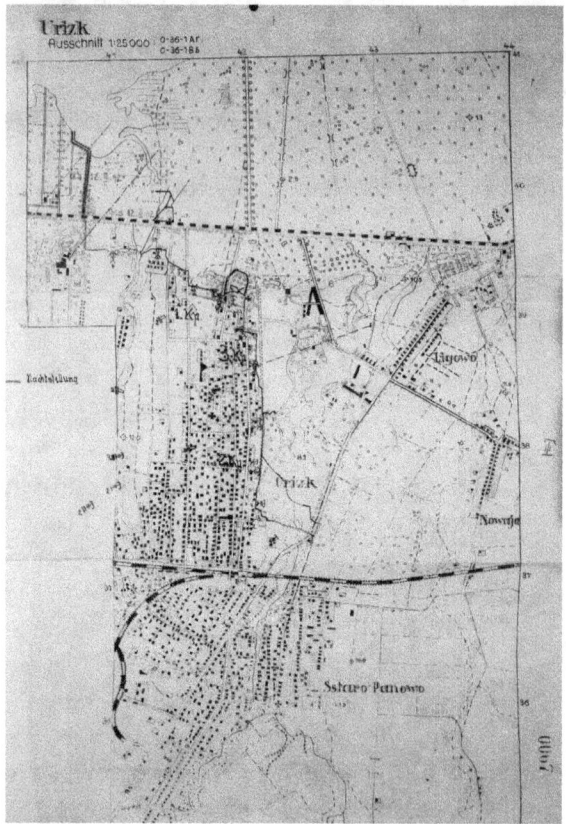

Detailed map of Urizk and the deployment of the Battalion's three companies in eastern border of the town.

On February 27, the *Wachbattalion* relieved the departing 158. *Infanterie-Regiment* and the *58. Infantrie-Division's Recon Battalion* on the front line. The trenches inherited would run from the ice-covered coast to 6 Kilometers inland along the completely leveled and burned remains of the old Leningrad workers town of Urzik. The area resembled a frozen and snowed in lunar landscape. The trenches ranged from adequately deep on their right flank to barely enough to crawl, nearing the coast. The enemy lines on their front would range from 300 meters away near the coast to barely 50 meters in the middle of the battalion's set up. Right in front of them was the burned-out ruins of a tall old military barrack that was occasionally used as a sniper hideout from which the Soviets would fire down into the shallow German trenches. From the battalion's lines, they could see the beached remains of the German heavy cruiser, *'Lützow'*. This ship had been sold to the Russians in 1940 but was never completed before being disabled as a floating battery by German heavy artillery in September 1941. The first week in line was spent improving the trenches and fortifications. The unit got 18 horses transferred for local service. Soon enough they were hailed through Soviet megaphones, telling them to remember the Soviets had reconquered Rostov and how like their *LSSAH* brethren they too would also soon be killed. The local artillery and mortar fire was intermittent these first weeks but sharpshooters would cause them grief and inflict mounting casualties.

Barbed wire obstacles in front of the *V./LSSAH* trenches at Urizk.   **German soldier with *MP-38*.**

Work at the barbed wire entanglements.

Artillery positions of the heavy batteries left behind at Urizk by the departing *58.Inf.Division*.

After a probing nocturnal patrol along the coast on March 14, a coup de main was staged by the battalion on the opposing Soviet bunker system. The assault was made by 20 men from the *1. Komp.* and some support assault engineers from the *5. (Schw.) Komp.* An 80-meter bunker complex was demolished and an estimated 20 Red Army soldiers killed by the time the assault group retreated at 03:40hrs in the morning. Their own casualties amounted to one man lightly wounded and several men debilitated with frostbite. Nothing much happened in the next two weeks aside routine trench life and artillery exchanges. By this time, Hugo Kraas, used to his *LSSAH* Reconnaissance Battalion's élan through the Ukraine that past year, was growing ever frustrated with the given task in this static backwater theatre surrounded by their inexperienced neighbors. It was not the first time that his superior, Jecklen, had ordered him to provide officers and NCOs to train the nearby police battalions on how to handle machine guns and other similar matters.

Two heavily dressed SS men with their issue *Schneehemde*, typical for the first winter.

German soldiers in a Russian village, Winter 1941/42.

Light machine gunner in position in the trenches.

Ruins of Urizk, February 1942.

Annoyed with his lot he wrote to Sepp Dietrich, his *LSSAH* divisional commander back in south Ukraine, complaining how much administrative paperwork he had to endure here, how he had to continuously send men and materiel to his terribly equipped and ill trained neighbor units, providing scarce manpower to guard the munitions depots, handle the supply dumps and help in the various new headquarters detachments. Bemoaning all his vehicles being confiscated for the *Kampfgruppen's* use, his battalion gunsmith and his spare parts being carted away and on top of it, how the *Wachbattalion* had to furnish a personal guard to Friedrich Jeckeln himself. With the coming of the end of March, the snow and ice that had been used to bolster the shallow trenches started to melt making life miserable in the flooded fortifications and exposing the defenders to more enemy fire.

Heavy Machinegun position overlooking the plain in front of Leningrad from Urizk.

Picture of some volunteers of the Norwegian SS Battalion which was to take over the *V./LSSAH* positions at Urizk after its departure towards the town of Mga.

Positions near Apraskin where the *V./LSSAH* was to deploy along the old trenches of the *223.Inf.Division.*

The good news was that Kraas' letters to Dietrich seem to have hit home and orders arrived to get the stranded unit out of this perceived inglorious service. Since the middle of March, the 54th Soviet Army had tried to reach the now cut off 2nd Shock Army in the Volkhov swamps from its north east. This new offensive had been met with stiff German resistance and had been stopped thus far after some initial Soviet gains. The *Wachbattalion* was to be taken out of the *Kampfgruppe Jeckeln* by the personal order of Hitler and sent eastwards to act as combat reserve near where the danger was more serious. Orders arrived on the 29th of March and by the 30th the battalion was relieved by the Norwegian Legion. The remaining 14 horses were handed over along with the artillery pieces that had been left with unit from the *58. Infanterie-Division* upon its arrival. The companies mustered and were ferried during the night in two truck convoys to the town of Mga, to the south east of Leningrad. Once there, Kraas received instructions to stand by with his unit, rest it and undergo training in infantry tank hunting tactics. The battalion got attached to the local *223. Infanterie-division* and their time was also spent visiting the nearby front lines to familiarize themselves with it. After a week doing this, radio orders were received on April 8 to ready the battalion for immediate train transfer 20 Kms to the south east and have it to be attached to the 333. *Infanterie-Regiment*. Intelligence had been received that the Soviet 54th Army was to renew its offensive towards the desperate cut off 2nd Shock Army. The *Wachbattalion* was to be sent into action there. On the next day, the order was countermanded and instead the unit was to relieve two battalions from the 223. ID which would instead be sent to the fight in its place.

Pictures of the swampy conditions of the new positions of the Battalion on the train route from Mga to Vologda and Tikhvin. Heavy destruction and numerous soviet tank wrecks attest to the heavy fighting that had taken place in the area in the past months.

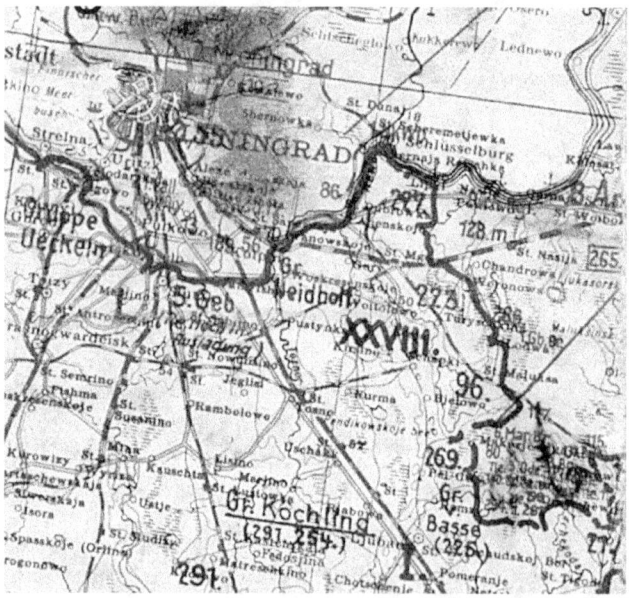

General map of the area of operations. Near the gulf of Finland on the west of Leningrad one can find the Kampfgruppe Jecklen deployed with the 50th Army Korps while to the east we can find the 28th Army Korps with the *223.Infanterie-Division* where the *V./LSSAH* would move on April 1942 till June.

By the 12th the unit had set up along the Mga-Volkhov-Tikhvin rail line near the ruins of the small villages of Apraskin, Mishkino and Tortolowo. The landscape had suffered grievously in the continuous fighting around the area as the 54th Soviet Army had repeatedly tried to break through the front to reach Leningrad in the fall of 1941. Taking over the recently vacated trench lines in the swamps and forests on both sides of the rail line, the *Wachbattalion* settled in. Soon they would realize that not much had changed from being in front of Leningrad. Bunker systems on both sides, heavy wire entanglements and minefields separated both enemies. During the daytime, activity was minimal aside from occasional sniper fire and the scattered artillery exchange while the troops mostly kept to their living bunkers and out of sight. During the night times, things would liven up as flares flew overhead and machineguns would rake the barbed wire entanglements at the smallest suspicion or noise. Disabled tanks dotted the landscape and some T34s left within the German lines from previous assaults were used as fixed artillery positions by the troops to fire on the Russians. One tank was even repaired to working condition and used by the battalion to drive up and down the lines as extra fire support.

Heavy destruction and numerous soviet tank wrecks....

The next two weeks passed in this manner as the frost thawed turning everything into a huge ankle-deep sea of mud. Supplies were brought up to Apraskin, in their rearguard, by train and from there they had to be laboriously carried up by hand to the trenches. Bunkers collapsed as the frost disappeared and continuous improvement works kept everyone busy. Mosquitos also came back with a vengeance and living without a protective net became a nightmare. The thawing also affected the multitude of Soviet corpses between the lines that added to the general misery of trench warfare. Nightly throwing of chlorine to ward of the nauseous smell had little effect. On April 24th, the 2. *Komp.* launched a coup de main against the opposing bunker system which ended with several fortifications and living quarters blown up with no personal loss. Trench life continued as described for a month without any telltale event of importance.

On May 23rd, a Soviet company-sized attack probed against the 3. *Komp.* on the right flank and was repulsed with small arms fire and the assistance of a called in artillery barrage. On the 28th a new, and stronger, Russian assault was staged against the 1. *Komp.* right in the center of the battalion's deployment along the railway line, this time with a preparatory artillery barrage, followed up with flamethrower carrying sappers clearing the barbed wire and opening a passage across the minefield. This attack was also repulsed with the timely help of the German artillery. Around 50 to 60 dead and wounded Soviet soldiers were left between the lines.

Swampy misery for logistics as everything had to be brought up by hand to the positions.

Mosquito nets became a must as the snow and ice gave way to ankle deep mud everywhere.

While the battalion was busy repairing the barbed wire and placing new mines, orders arrived from the *XXVI Armee Korp* instructing the unit to get ready to be moved out of the line. The next couple of days saw much grapevine talk as to what their next assignment would be. Finally, on the night of the 5th of June the companies filed out while the 223. ID took over again its old lines. Right in the middle of this exchange another Soviet attack took place which was easily repulsed. Having reached the nearby town of Mga, the Battalion started to repair gear, clean up, rest, practice sports and attend theoretical lessons until the June 9th. On the 10th, they all boarded a waiting train and started their march south.

As at Urizk, Police Battalions became once again the neighbors of the *V./LSSAH* south of the Ladoga sea.

On February 28th, the battalion entered the lines at Urzik with 24 officers, 124 noncommissioned officers and 887 enlisted ranks. During the 103 days with Army Group North the *Wachbattalion* would lose 71 dead, comprising 3 officers, 4 NCOs and 64 enlisted ranks. To these figures we must add 128 wounded that would not return to the unit, comprising 4 officers, 12 NCOs and 112 enlisted ranks. Additionally, 76 men would have to be further detracted due to sickness, frostbite and transfers. When the train left the station of Mga it had 18 officers, 95 NCOs and 647 enlisted ranks on board.

On June 17th, the *V./LSSAH Wachbattalion* convoy reached Stalino in southern Ukraine. Here the rest of the *Leibstandarte* was gathering from the winter frontline positions around Sambek, to rest, refurbish and consolidate into a full division. On the 19th the replacement and training battalion that had been sent in the previous February to the Sennelager camp also arrived to join them.

Between the 3rd and the 10th of July, the division would reorganize with the *V./LSSAH Wachbattalion* joining the veteran LSSAH II. and IV. Battalions and forming the new 2nd Inf. Rgt. LSSAH under command of *SS-Obersturmbannführer* Theodor Wisch, who had previously led with success the *II./LSSAH*. *SS-Hstuf.* Hugo Kraas would keep commanding his *V./LSSAH Wachbattalion*, which would be renamed as First Battalion of the new Second Regiment. He would keep commanding this unit till April of the next year, where after the successful campaign around Kharkov he would replace Wisch as commander of the 2nd Regiment. While Hans Becker, who had lead his second company, while around Leningrad, would take his position in turn and lead the Battalion. Both would also earn the Knights Cross for those combats in the spring of 1943. But that was still almost a year away and first they were all to be sent to France to fully reorganize, refit, train and eventually become a full Panzer Grenadier Division.

Bibliography

Kriegstagebuch V./LSSAH - T-354 R-610 National Archives, graciously provided by Carol Byrne
Rudolf Lehmann, *Die Leibstandarte. Juli 1941 bis Januar 1943. Band II*, Nation Europa Verlag, 1995
Charles Trang, *Leibstandarte 1933 – 1943*, Editions Heimdal, 2007
Charles Trang, *Dictionnaire de la Leibstandarte*, Editions Heimdal, 2010

Hungarian Armored Forces in WW2
by Eduardo Manuel Gil Martínez
(Translated by José Antonio Muñoz Molero)

Hungarian Light Tanks CV-33, Cluj Autumn 1940.

Introduction

The performance of the armoured forces of Germany's allied countries during the Second World War is quite unknown even for the fans of the history of the Second World War. Although it is true that the performance of these was usually quite secondary when not disappointing, it would be worth remember the courageous behavior of the Hungarian armoured forces. In recent times, authors such as Péter Mujzer, Czaba Becze, Clotier or Bernád and Climent have delved into this topic, providing a lot of information about it. We will try in this text to review the highlights of the intervention of the Magyar armoured forces during the Second World War.

38M Toldi belonging to a light tank Company belonging to cavalry forces in Transylvania in 1940. Courtesy of Péter Mujzer.

The Hungarian rearmament

At the end of the World War I (WWI), the Austro-Hungarian Empire was disbanded in several countries, being subject to the conditions of the Treaty of Versailles in 1919 and mutilated various areas belonging to the Austrian territory by the Treaty of Trianon in 1920. The Hungarian armed forces were radically limited in quantity and in the quality of their materials; besides Hungary lost part of Transylvania (which passed to Romania), Rijeka, Slovakia, Croatia, Vojvodina or Bosnia-Herzegovina. The situation worsened more for Hungary when in the 1930s all its neighbors (Czechoslovakia, Romania or Yugoslavia) reassembled in much greater amount to theirs, leaving partially surrounded and helpless to Hungary. In 1934, Hungary improved its war potential with the acquisition of 150 tankettes CV-33 Fiat-Ansaldo of Italian origin and 12 armoured vehicles Fiat L2.

These Ansaldo tankettes belonging to 2nd Reconnaissance Battalion somewhere in Transylvania in 1940 show us why the national emblem was not much appreciated among the crews. They were a real mobile "target". (*Péter Mujzer*).

Picture where we can see a row with four 35M Ansaldo in a village occupied in the Carpathians area where the movement of troops can be appreciated. (*Károly Németh*).

One Csaba passes a Hungarian road control in the front. Courtesy of Péter Mujzer.

Simultaneously, emerges the figure of Nicholas Strausser, a Hungarian who designed an armoured vehicle based on the Alvis C2 armed with a 20 mm cannon, which was called Csaba. The Honved (Royal Hungarian Army) placed an order of 100 units of this fast armoured manufactured by the Hungarian industry *Manfred Weiss*.

First blood

In 1938 as a result of Germany's territorial demands on Czechoslovakia, Hungary took the opportunity to claim part of its lost territories during the WWI. Without reaching the confrontation during the days 5-10 of November of the same year the historically Hungarian northern territories were occupied peacefully by four infantry bodies with a total of seven companies of platforms. After that, the new objective Magyar was Ruthenian (part of the territory that also having been Hungarian, became integrated in Czechoslovakia) despite the German Reich was shown against the Hungarian intentions. The campaign began on March 15, 1939 with the advancement of the moving body and the VIII moving body. The Hungarian onslaught against the enemy troops was so fast, that on the 17th the companies equipped with Hungarian Ansaldo tankettes reached the Polish border. In ten days, the Hungarian objectives were achieved. In these actions in Czechoslovakia it was possible to see that much of the Ansaldo tankettes had not been able to resist a clash against a powerful enemy and for less than two weeks. Mechanical problems, breaks and lack of spare material, completely decimated those armored vehicles.

The commander of a Toldi I poses for the camera. The tricolor octagonal emblem and a white eagle of a cavalry armoured battalion are clearly seen in both the hatch and the side of the vehicle. Courtesy of Károly Németh.

The Toldi I on muddy ground complied adequately, but its scarce armor damaged its design in general. Courtesy of Péter Mujzer.

World War II begins

At the beginning of the WWII, the Hungarian Army consisted of 9 Corps, 1 Mobile Corp, 25 divisions and 18 regiments, as well as other mixed frontier units, etc. Among them deserves special attention the Mobile Corp, which was the core of the Army which included two motorized brigades and two cavalry brigades apart from other minor units. Hungary took advantage of the situation to improve its strategic situation, being its new objective Transylvania, in Romanian possession after the Treaty of Trianon. In the summer of 1940 the territory was claimed to the Romanian Government, obtaining its occupation between November 5 and 13. The armoured vehicles that intervened in this "peaceful" occupation, consisted of the obsolete Ansaldo, the tanks 38 M Toldi (40 in total) and the armoured car M39 Csaba (13 in total), newly incorporated to the Hungarian Army and the pride of the National war industry. Despite not participating in any combat, the difficult of the terrain required an urgent maintenance work of the Ansaldo, Toldi and Csaba. In the spring of 1941 Hungary as a result of his adherence to the Axis, participated in the German invasion of Yugoslavia, supporting its ally. The Hungarian participation was by means of the III Hungarian Army (composed of the I, IV and V Corps and the Mobile Corp) that began its advance on April 11 in direction to the Danube in the Baranya (only 5 days before the bulk of the German troops had begun the attack on Yugoslavia). In the Mobile Corp again participated the 38 M Toldi and 39 Csaba that joined the outdated 35M Ansaldo.

Major General Béla Dálnoki Miklós, second from the Left, 1941.

The campaign in the USSR of 1941

Initially Hungary did not participate in Operation Barbarossa initiated on June 22, 1941 against the Soviet Union, but after the supposed Soviet bombardment of the Hungarian cities of Kassa and Munkacs on June 26, the war was declared with the USSR on June 27. It was on June 27th, 1941 when the Hungarian troops of the so-called "Carpathians" Group composed by the Mobile Corp (known as *Gyorshadtest*), the 1st Mountain Brigade and the 8th Border Brigade began to move towards Soviet territory from the front of the Carpathians, being integrated into the 17th German army. The *Gyorshadtest* was assigned to the area of Huzst-Marmarossziget-Borkut under the command of Major General Béla Dálnoki Miklós and had 75-80% of its optimum potential: 81 38 m Toldi I, 60 35M Ansaldo and 48 39 Csaba (later would be added 14 Toldi, 5 Ansaldo tankettes and 9 Csaba to replace vehicles that were out of work.

A couple of Pz 38 in a village during its advance through Soviet lands. Despite representing an important step for the Magyar armoured forces, it was obsolete at the time of acquiring it to the Germans. Courtesy of Péter Mujzer.

The Mobile Corp in June 29, 1941 was composed of:

• 1st Motorized Brigade (under the command of Major General Jenö major).

• 2nd Motorized Brigade. (Major General János Vörös).

• 1st Cavalry Brigade. (Major General Antal Vattay).

• Other minor units.

Each of the two motorized brigades that were part of the Mobile Corp, had 36 38 m Toldi I and 16 reconnaissance vehicles 39 Csaba; the 1st Cavalry Brigade in fulfilling reconnaissance missions was only endowed with 9 38 m Toldi I and 36 35M Ansaldo.

Hungarian *PzKpfw.IV Ausf F-1* in Russia, 1942.

A Pz IV F1 column belonging the company of heavy tanks from the Magyar Tank Battalion advance by Soviet lands during the campaign of 1942. Courtesy of Péter Mujzer.

A Hungarian soldier close to an Italian made Ansaldo tankette. Courtesy of Károly Németh and Péter Mujzer.

After taking the mountain passes of the Carpathians in Panter and Tatár will be the *Gyorshadtest* that would bear the bulk of the progress in the region of Galitzia to progress through Ukrainian territory. The advance began very slowly because of the resistance of the Soviets. When the mountain paths were left behind Hungarian forces, was therefore when the *Gyorshadtest* began to show its real possibilities of deepening in the immensity of the USSR. On July 7, they crossed the Dniester, leaving the *Gyorshadtest* under the command of the German Army Group South under the command of Marshal von Rundstedt. Belonging to 17th German Army, the Gyorshadtest participated in the march to Kiev. After this, the *Gyorshadtest* was assigned to the 1st German Panzer Group aiming at the Stalin line. The Hungarians destroyed a number of Soviet vehicles and captured at least 13 tanks and 12 artillery pieces, breaking the Soviet defensive line. The Hungarian casualties were 6 *38 m Toldi I* destroyed and 7 damaged, leaving out of service 3 *39 Csaba*. The Hungarian armoured forces were a tough rival for the Soviets especially because of the obsolete of the Soviet armoured ones (*BT-2, BT-5, BT-7, T-26, T-37* and *T-38*). Between the 22nd and the 29th of July, the *Gyorshadtest* was in tasks of cleaning of the

Soviet troops still positioned west of the river Bug, 32 *Toldi* and 18 *Ansaldo* were lost. To compensate for the high number of casualties in the armoured units, the 27th of July, were sent from Hungary by railway, 14 *38 Toldi I*, 9 *39 Csaba* and 5 *35M Ansaldo*.

A Nimród participating in an anti-aircraft fire exercise, though shortly thereafter would prove his worth as an armoured weapon. Courtesy of Károly Németh.

Hungarian reconnaissance vehicle 39 Csaba on the Eastern Front, Summer 1942.

A command Toldi followed by a medevac Toldi cross a river during the campaign of 1942. Courtesy of Péter Mujzer.

At the end of July, the *Gyorshadtest* was in the south-west of Umán, west of the River Bug, collaborating with the German troops in the enclosure of important Soviet units (the 6th and 12th Soviet armies) in what would be called the Umán pocket. On August 8, the besieged Soviet forces (about 100000 men) surrendered definitively. Later the Gyorshadtest would participate in the offensive towards Nikolayev, which was achieved on August 17. After that, he was entrusted with the mission of taking positions on the right bank of the river Dnieper along about 200 Km just to the left of the 3rd Romanian Army. In the upper echelons of Hungarian Army began to doubt the permanence in the front of its troops. To force the Germans to accept this new strategy, any kind of maintenance or replacement of the lost vehicles was prevented during the Gyorshadtest campaign. Finally, in a staggered manner, the different Magyar units were repatriated, and the Gyorshadtest remained active until November 24.

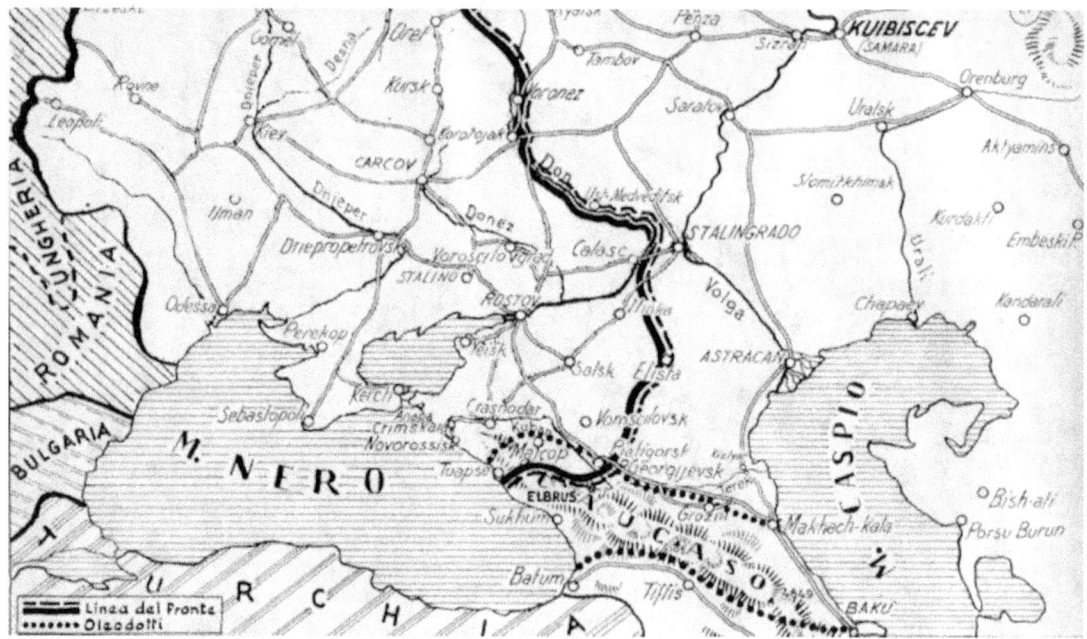

Don Front, Summer-Autumn 1942. The Soviet bridgeheads on the Don River at Uryv and Korotoyak, were at south of Voronezh.

Impressive picture showing a group of the Magyar armored force with numerous Pz 38 and Nimród ready for action. Courtesy of Károly Németh.

1942. Return to Ukraine

During the beginning of 1942, the Hungarian participation in the Eastern Front was limited to occupation units acting in the rear; but Germany demanded the aid from Hungary in the battles of the Eastern Front. After many negotiations, the Hungarians offered their 2nd Army. This new Magyar unit had some 200000 men and was gathered under the command of Colonel General Gusztav Jany. 2nd Army was constituted by three Army Corps (III Corps composed of 6th, 7th and 9th Infantry Divisions, the fourth Corp composed of 10th, 12th and 13th Infantry Divisions and the VII Corp composed of 19th, 20th and 23rd Infantry Divisions), the 1st Armoured Division and several independent units. The Hungarian armoured forces had better armoured ones like the Panzer 38 (Pz 38 or Skoda 38 (t)), the Panzer I and IV F-1 and the light Toldi tanks. The spearhead of the 1st Armoured Division was the 30th Armoured Regiment consisting of two battalions. Each battalion had a company of heavy tanks with 11 PZ IV F-1, 3 PZ 38 and 1 38 m Toldi; and two medium tank companies with 20 Pz 38 each one. In addition, several ambulance and command vehicles were added. Its total strength was 104 Pz 38, 22 Pz IV F-1, 6 Toldi and 6 Pz I. In addition to the 30th Armoured Regiment, we must highlight the presence of other armoured vehicles in the 2nd Army as the 40M Nimrod anti-aircraft armored and the 39 Csaba armoured cars.

Csaba armoured car in Ukraine, Summer 1942.

Pz IV F1 maneuvering by a dislevel. This combat tank was the first truly comparable to its opponents of those who arranged the Magyar armoured forces. Courtesy of Károly Németh.

The 2nd Hungarian Army was ordered to control a sector of the river Don bank, arriving on July 7 to its deployment zone of about 200 kilometers of the West bank of the river Don; leaving the armored in second line to be considered as the reserve of the 2nd Army. At that time, in the western sector of the river the Soviets still had three bridgeheads: in Uryv, Korotyak and in Shchuche (Shchuchye); that were very dangerous to be in direct contact with the Hungarian positions. The order of Battle of the 1st Armoured Division at this time, was the following (according to Stenge and Cloutier):

30º Armoured Regiment.
30/I Armoured Battalion (with its companies 30/1, 30/2 and 30/3).
30/II Armoured Battalion (with its companies 30/4, 30/5 and 30/6).

1st Brigade of Motorized riflemen.
1st Motorized riflemen Battalion.
2nd Motorized riflemen Battalion.
3rd Motorized riflemen Battalion.
51 º self-propelled Anti-Aircraft Battalion.

One Nimrod with its full crew during maneuvers. Courtesy of Károly Németh.

1st Motorized Signal Battalion.
1st Motorized medium howitzers Battalion.
5th Motorized medium howitzers Battalion.
2nd Anti-Aircraft Battalion.
1st Reconnaissance Battalion.
1st Sapper Company.
1st Traffic Control Company.
1st Power Supply Battalion.

During this period various clashes were held where the Hungarian armoured faced the Soviets in the bridgeheads in Uryv and Korotoyak.

First Battle of Uryv

On 18 July, the 7th Light Division supported by the 30/I Armoured Battalion, the 51 º self-propelled Anti-Aircraft Battalion and the 1st Motorized riflemen Battalion began the attack against the Soviet troops belonging to 24th Soviet Armoured Corps (which had more than 100 tanks among which were the powerful T-34/76 as well as T-60, KV-1 and M3 Stuart). In this attack the Hungarians managed to put out of combat 21 enemy armoured vehicles mainly thanks to the Pz IV. In this combat the 40 m anti-aircraft Nimrod showed that their utility could also encompass land combat. After the first day of fighting, the Hungarians had managed to eliminate the Soviets from the bridgehead, but the Soviet counteroffensive did not wait and that same night they managed to resume their positions in Uryv returning the Hungarians to their initial positions on July 20th.

One of the Pz III M received by Hungary in September 1942 to try to overcome the immense casualties suffered in the Don combat front. Courtesy of Károly Németh.

First Battle of Korotoyak

Immediately after the finish of the Battle of Uryv, the Hungarian Command decided on an attack on Korotoyak. Again the bulk of the attack would take the 1st Armoured Division reinforced by the exhausted 12th Light Division. The Hungarians used 103 Pz 38, 20 Pz IV, 12 40 m Nimrod, 7 38, Toldi, as well as seven anti-tank cannons. On August 7th at six in the morning the armoured troops advanced to the Don, but the enemy resistance was so tenacious that they managed to resist. The next day, an attack carried out by 20 Soviet tanks was repelled by destroying four of them. After this the Hungarian tanks were used as assault artillery in order to eliminate the

Soviet resistance zones; succeeding partially to date of August 9. The 1st Armoured Division lost after this combat 38 Pz 38, 2 Pz IV and 2 38M Toldi. After these battles, a 1st Armoured Division was urgently claimed in Uryv.

One of the first Pz IV F2 in Hungarian hands. Compared to the F1 model, its fire capacity was greatly improved. Courtesy of Károly Németh.

Command tank 1st Armoured Division, 1942.

Second Battle of Uryv

On August 10th, the Hungarians led by the 1st Armoured Division and the 13th Light Division began a new attack, which proved unlucky. The result was in the first moment the stop of the advance and shortly after the withdrawal towards the starting line of the Hungarian attack.

Second Battle of Korotoyak

During August 8th and 9th a new Soviet offensive took place from Korotoyak bridgehead. The only Hungarian armoured vehicles were those belonging to 30/II Armoured Battalion, which managed to stop the Soviet advance. After completing the second battle in Uryv the 1st Armoured Division returned to the vicinity of Korotoyak, which allowed a backlash on August 15. On this day at least 10 Soviet tanks were destroyed (T-60 and M3); and on August 18 the front line stabilized. After the second Battle of Korotoyak were in service for the combat only 55 Pz 38, 15 Pz IV. The worn out and tired Hungarian troops led the Germans to reinforce the first Armoured Division with four Pz IV F2, which were received at the end of August. Towards the first of September the 1st Armoured Division thanks to the reinforcements coming from the Germans and to the repair and commissioning of some cars, rose to 85 Pz 38, 22 Pz IV (F1 and F2) and 5 38MToldi.

PzKpfw 38(t) Ausf D of the *1st Armored Division.*

Nimrod in action, Autumn 1942.

Hungarian soldiers on the Eastern Front, Autumn 1942.

Third Battle of Uryv

On September 9, a new German-Hungarian attack was launched against the Uryv bridgehead, acting the 1st Armoured Division across the front line. In this clash, several combat tanks Pz IV F-1 and PZ 38 were lost in front of the Soviet armoured ones. On the 11th, finally, thanks to the effort of Hungarians and Germans, Stotozhevoye is taken. At the end of day 12, they were only kept ready to combat 4 Pz IV and 22 Pz 38. These tanks the next day managed to destroy 8 T-34 tanks and damage 2 KV-1 in a new Soviet offensive. On the 16th, a new Soviet attack was halted, after which the third Battle of Uryv ended. The 1st Hungarian Armoured Division only had at this time 2 Pz IV F-1 and 12 Pz-38, so it was to be removed from combat line. To compensate for the important Hungarian casualties and to recompose the 1st Armoured Division, the Germans agreed to deliver them in October of 1942, 10 Pz IV F-2, 10 Pz III M and possibly between 4 and 8 Pz II F. In December 10, StuG III N Germans with German crews would be subordinate to the Hungarians.

Bibliography
Gil Martínez, Eduardo Manuel. *Fuerzas acorazadas húngaras 1939-45.* Almena. 2017.

Italian Eastern Front Awards
by Rene Chavez

Illustrated above is a very nice and scarce WW2 Alpini hat with a M37 pattern eagle insignia. The number "8" attached to the insignia indicate that it belong to the 8th Alpini Regiment of the Julia Division. Below is a 1939 dagger with three rivet wooden handle and black scabbard normally used by Italian Paratroopers and black militias. In the center is the C.S.I.R. cross.

Italian Alpini.

Corpo di Spedizione Italiano in Russia Messe Document

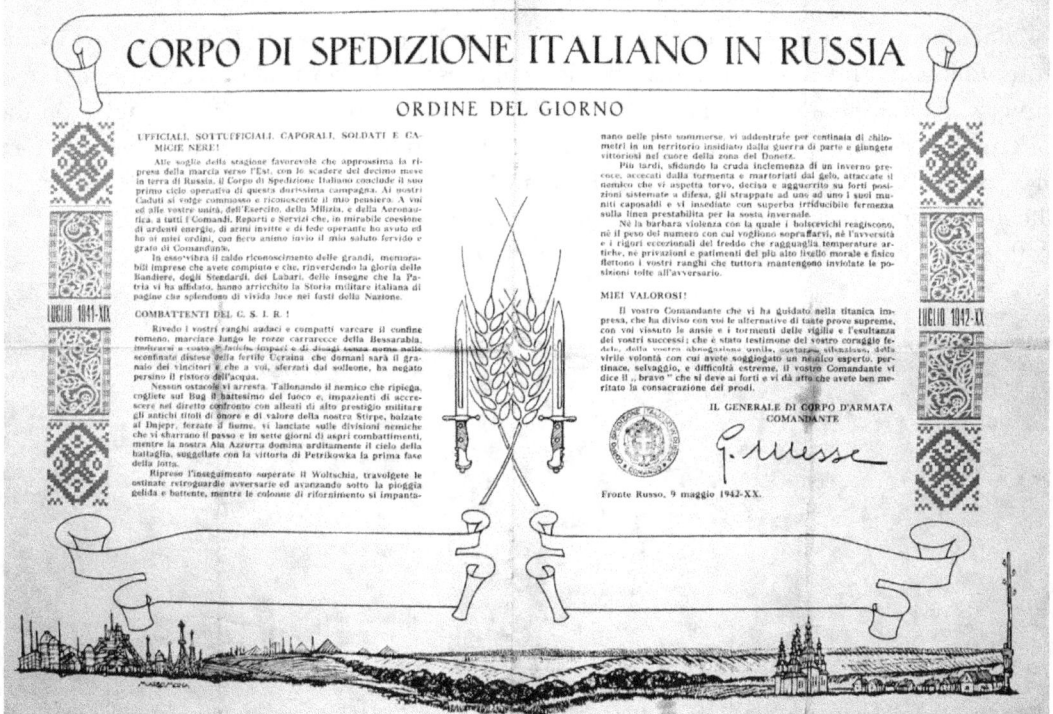

C.S.I.R. document written by General Messe to his men declaring a final farewell and officially recognizing them for their heroic acts in battle while serving under his command in Russia. This document was issued to his troops in the summer of 1942.

General Messe with Italian soldiers of C.S.I.R. on Eastern Front, Spring 1942.

The document has a C.S.I.R. circular seal with the House of Savoy Coat of Arms in the center follow by the facsimile signature General Messe. The document was designed by a former C.S.I.R. veteran Lieutenant Colonel Mario Mona who posted his signature on the bottom lower left side of the document. On the bottom right side has the printer's information "SA Grafitalia via Pizzi & Pythian Milano Rome." Mona was attached in the elite Bersaglieri, he went missing in action in Livorno on July 12--13, 1943. He was posthumously awarded the gold medal for military valor.

The general Messe inspects a C.S.I.R. unit, Spring 1942.

Italian soldiers in Russia, 1942.

An alpine in winter camouflage in Russia, 1942.

Italian CSIR Cross

Italian C.S.I.R. award was probably instituted in August 1942 and rendered to those troops that participated in the initial campaign of Operation Barbarossa. The cross is made of either silver, silver bronze or silver zama. The obverse is found in either off-white paint or enameled surrounded by a metal border outline. The reverse has the names of the Russian regions and the years that the Italian troops fought. In addition, the manufacturer's name and address is posted on the lower right side. For the silver cross an "800" mark is posted on the lower left corner side. The Ribbon is white and black.

Above is an original white painted cross with silver metal outlines attached to a white/black ribbon.

General Messe and Duce Benito Mussolini on Eastern Front.

Detail of the inscriptions.

Notice that the reverse shows the names of the Russian regions and the years that the Italian troops fought.

On top of the cross, is the inscription "DNJEPR, DONETZ" and on the bottom, is the dates "LUGLIO 941, LUGLIO 942." Perpendicular to the cross, from left to right, the inscription "BUG" and "DON." In the center, it shows the "C.S.I.R." in large size letters.

In addition, just below the date, it shows in small letters the manufacturer's name and address "LORIOLI MILANO ROMA, A PICOZZI MILANO.".

Post-production badges exist probably made and purchased for veterans. The post-war crosses are missing the manufacturer's name and address.

Italian FRONTE-RUSSO Badge

The so-called Italian FRONTE-RUSSO honor badge was awarded in March 1943 to all those troops that served on the Eastern Front from 22 June 1941 to 5 June 1943. The badge was also awarded to Germans attached to the C.S.I.R. and 8th Army Corps. This attractive silver color badge shows the wreath with laurels (representing heroism) on the right side and thorns (representing suffering) on the left side, both touching the knot of Savoy at the top. The center of the badge shows two Cossack sabers crossing. At the base is a ribbon with the inscription "FRONTE RUSSO" highlighted in blue. On the reverse of the badge was the name and address of the manufacturing company "F. M. LORIOLI FRATELLI, VIA F. BRONZETTI 25, MILANO" and the manufacturing pattern number "MODELLO DEPOSITATO NO. 38." The badge was attached to the left pocket of the uniform via a pin. This die cast badge was sold for 6 Lira and was available directly from the only authorized manufacturing company the Lorioli Brothers. It came with a brown cellophane paper showing the manufacturer's logo and address.

There exist two versions on the badge the difference is shown on the reverse. Above is a rare early issued Fronte - Russo badge. This badge has a needle pin with a catch and hinge that was placed in vertical position, which was later removed and replaced by a safety pin that follow the contour lines of the saber as shown in the second version.

Italian CSIR Cross

Troops of the Italian Expeditionary Forces in Russia were awarded with a black enameled cross for their participation on the Russian Front. The black cross shown on the top right side has the golden Italian Royal Eagle with the Arms of Savoy in the center and the inscription "C.S.I.R." (Corpo di Spedizione Italiano in Russia) just below the wings.

Italian CSIR Cross.   **German and Italian troops in a trench, Russia Autumn 1941.**

The ribbon shows the Italian national colors: green/white/red. Italian medals were actually required to be purchased by the recipient for a small fee.

Decorated soldiers of the *Pasubio* division, Russia Autumn-Winter 1941/42.

Bibliography

Rene Chavez, *Foreign Volunteerlegion* - <u>Web Site</u>: www.foreignvolunteerlegion.com

in World War Two 1939-1945

WW2 AXIS FORCES

www.ingramcontent.com/pod-product-compliance
Lightning Source LLC
Chambersburg PA
CBHW081723120626
46550CB00010B/3231